LAID OFF, LAID LOW

*The Columbia University Press and Social Science Research Council
Series on the Privatization of Risk*

THE COLUMBIA UNIVERSITY PRESS AND
SOCIAL SCIENCE RESEARCH COUNCIL
SERIES ON THE PRIVATIZATION OF RISK

Edited by Craig Calhoun and Jacob S. Hacker

The early twenty-first century is witnessing a concerted effort to privatize risk—to shift responsibility for the management or mitigation of key risks onto private-sector organizations or directly onto individuals. This series uses social science research to analyze this issue in depth. Each volume presents a concise review of a particular topic from the perspective of the public and private allocation of risk and responsibility and offers analysis and empirical, evidence-based opinion from leading scholars in the fields of economics, political science, sociology, anthropology, and law. Support for the series comes from the John D. and Catherine T. MacArthur Foundation.

Jacob S. Hacker, ed., *Health at Risk: America's Ailing Health System—and How to Heal It*

Andrew Lakoff, ed., *Disaster and the Politics of Intervention*

Donald W. Light, ed., *The Risks of Prescription Drugs*

Mitchell A. Orenstein, ed., *Pensions, Social Security, and the Privatization of Risk*

Laid Off, Laid Low

Political and Economic Consequences
of Employment Insecurity

EDITED BY KATHERINE S. NEWMAN

COLUMBIA UNIVERSITY PRESS | NEW YORK

A COLUMBIA/SSRC BOOK

COLUMBIA UNIVERSITY PRESS
Publishers Since 1893
New York   Chichester, West Sussex

Copyright © 2008 Columbia University Press

Library of Congress Cataloging-in-Publication Data

Laid off, laid low : economic and political consequences of
employment insecurity / edited by Katherine S. Newman.
     p.   cm.—(The Columbia University Press
and Social Science Research Council series on the
privatization of risk)
    ISBN 978-0-231-14604-3 (cloth : alk. paper)—
    ISBN 978-0-231-14605-0 (pbk. : alk. paper)—
    ISBN 978-0-231-51862-8 (e-book)
    1. Job security—United States. 2. Unemployment—
United States. 3. United States—Economic conditions
—2001– I. Newman, Katherine S., 1953– II. Title.
III. Series.

 HD5708.45.U6.L35 2008
331.25'96—dc22

                       2008020482

References to Internet Web sites (URLs) were
accurate at the time of writing. Neither the
contributors nor Columbia University Press
is responsible for URLs that may have expired
or changed since the manuscript was prepared.

Design by Julie Fry
Cover by Vin Dang

CONTENTS

LAID OFF, LAID LOW

Introduction | *High Anxiety*

KATHERINE S. NEWMAN

By some measures, the American economy has been in high gear for the better part of two decades. The stock market soared well over the magic mark of 12,000 and stayed there for months until tumbling on the news of recession in early 2008. Unemployment remained below 5% for much of this decade. Yet storm clouds began gathering in late 2007. Housing markets tanked across the country; oil prices spiked to over $100 a barrel; and the dollar fell to historic lows, sending governments and private investors around the world scurrying to find safe havens elsewhere. The implosion of the subprime lending market and subsequent tailspin of the largest U.S. mortgage firms and major banks shook the financial markets. Firms went hat in hand to foreign lands in search of investors, leaving everything from landmark buildings to major industries in the hands of strangers.

American families sensed the instability in the air and the index of consumer confidence nose-dived in response. Presidential candidates who had been, only months before, fixated on the war in Iraq began to argue over the size of the stimulus package designed to ward off recession.

For the average family, the forest of economic indicators reviewed daily in the business press has only modest meaning. What the man and woman on main street cares about more than any other measure is the security of their jobs. Families can tighten their belts if prices rise: put off seeing the dentist, wear those old shoes another season, forgo the trip to Disneyland with the kids. But most Americans, save those in the very top income brackets, live close enough to the edge of their paychecks that the one thing they cannot absorb is prolonged unemployment. With less than two months of their annual incomes in savings, most families simply do not have the backstop they would need to withstand months without earnings. The most fortunate can borrow against the value of their homes if they hit a bad patch, but this is a risky strategy that can end up in foreclosure (as millions of Americans learned in 2007 alone). More common, and just as deadly, they can pull out the plastic, a practice that has led to skyrocketing rates of consumer debt. But none of these stop gap measures can really shore up a family if a pink slip turns into a long bout of joblessness.

And make no mistake: the proportion of American workers who face prolonged unemployment is growing. 463,000 jobs were cut from the national payroll in the first seven months of 2008. 3.7 million workers saw their hours cut to part time, "the largest figure since the government began tracking such data more than half a century ago."[1] The "R" word now appears regularly in the business press as the depth of the housing, credit, and financial market downturns becomes clear.

Since 1948, unemployment tended to peak near the end of recession and long-term unemployment (over twenty-seven weeks) crested not long thereafter. Typically this meant that it took about 1.6 months into an economic recovery for unemployment to start to come down and 8.3 months for those who were out of a job for a prolonged period to find their way back into the labor market. But starting in 2001, the picture changed in troubling ways. Unemployment now peaks much later (nineteen months) and long-term unemployment doesn't stop rising until two years after the official end of national recessions.[2]

Back in the "old days" when middle-class mothers didn't work, a family whose main breadwinner lost a job could send a second earner into the labor market to pick up some of the slack. Invariably the wife would earn less than her unemployed or underemployed husband, but the second income could become more than pin money. This is no longer a remedy for job loss in many American households because the wife is already at work and the family is consuming at a level that assumes both incomes. As Elizabeth Warren and Amelia Tyagi have shown in their much-cited book, *The Two Income Trap*,[3] middle- and working-class Americans are only able to manage when both parents are locked into the labor market.

It is no wonder, then, that families are more concerned with employment stability — his, hers, and theirs — than just about any other measure of well-being. Politicians know this all too well: incumbents can just about kiss their chances good-bye if the unemployment rate rises or the news of plant closings makes headlines in swing states. In a nation of wage earners, holding on to that paycheck is essential to survival in just about all classes save the very rich.

Scholars are aware of these concerns and hence from labor economics, to sociology, to political science, interest in *actual patterns* of employment instability, in *perceptions* of the risk of job loss, and the *political consequences* of these trends (real or imagined) is central. We want to know whether the landscape of employment stability has changed as inequality has increased, who has experienced the greatest change, whether these experiences matter in the sense of security that Americans in different occupational or income groups feel, and how (if at all), these patterns impact their political preferences.

In this short volume, the authors take a crack at all of these questions and the answers they offer paint a troubling, but important picture of a country that is both uncertain of its economic security and primed to let politicians know just how serious an issue this is through the power of the ballot box. Taken as an ensemble, the chapters in this volume point to an America in which the assumptions of the past no longer hold. It is not clear whether there is a new "system" in place, now that the twenty-year attachment to a single employer has become more of a rarity for prime-age workers. The anxieties about layoffs that were once confined to the boom/bust cycles of manufacturing, and the yearly experience of millions of blue-collar workers, are now a persistent headache for educated, white-collar managers. To be sure, the higher up the income hierarchy (and the credentials ladder), the less common layoffs and long-term unemployment become. But relative to the past, the rates of these unwelcome experiences have risen, even among the well-educated and highly skilled, and this translates into things that go bump in the night.

Globalization shadows the American economy in ways that ordinary Americans have had to reckon with directly since the passage of NAFTA. What began as a shift of jobs from unionized, high-wage regions of the United States to non-union states turned into a tidal wave of jobs moving offshore. When the trend impacted blue-collar jobs, states like Michigan and Pennsylvania felt the tremors. When it began to reach computer programmers or reservation clerks, whose jobs departed Silicon Valley for Bangalore, globalization became everyone's problem. With this genie out of the bottle, American workers have become anxious not only because it hits them in the pocketbook, but because the force of international competition seems beyond the control of domestic policy. Harsh anti-immigrant rhetoric is but one symptom of the ways in which globalization has added fuel to the fire of employment insecurity, whether or not immigrants are actually creating downward wage pressures, a matter of some controversy in economics.

This volume seeks to assess the impact of employment instability on the structure of careers, on perceptions of security, and on political preferences that are changing in response to objective and subjective instability. We begin with the most fundamental question: Has anything really changed in the last fifty years; that is, are American workers actually more vulnerable to job instability now than in the past? Henry Farber and Ann Huff Stevens come at this question with different data sets and appear, at times, to disagree on what their analyses have to say on this key point. Relying on the Current Population Survey from 1973 to 2006, Farber asks whether the probability of holding a job for twenty years or more has changed across the cohorts that have passed through their prime working years. He finds evidence of dramatic change: long-term employment relations have become less common and the proportion of male workers who have held their jobs for less than a year has increased sharply. Women, on the other hand, have seen little change in the duration of their jobs in the private sector.

Many years ago, Paul Osterman showed that churning is a natural and even beneficial practice because it helps new entrants to the labor market find the right fit and when they do, he pointed out, they tend to settle down into more stable patterns of employment.[4] Yet even then, it was clear that minorities, particularly young black men, were churning for many more years than more advantaged workers and that they bore "career scars," evidence of instability that warned employers off them. When the economy improved, as it did during the so-called "Massachusetts miracle"[5] or during the late 1990s and early part of this decade,[6] these scars were less consequential. Tight labor markets put pressure on employers to take a second look at job applicants they might have passed by in slack markets. In general, though, churning—particularly job hopping that does not lead to better pay and more responsibility, that is, to upward mobility—is problematic because it signals to employers that a worker is not reliable.

Farber identifies evidence of increased churning later in life than used to be the case. Where new entrants to the labor market once settled down in their early twenties, the job-hopping process is now extending into the early thirties, and that—almost by definition—limits the experience of long-term tenure. Whether this will become a secular trend that engulfs the entire labor force is a question upon which these two chapters do not converge. Farber sees a fundamental change that is increasingly sweeping the American work force; Stevens argues that it is still a minority experience, with long tenure the majority pattern, but agrees that it is more common among younger workers.

Stevens comes at the question of employment instability through several special surveys of older men begun in the late 1960s and constructs measures of the longest job a worker has ever held. Focusing on cohorts of men who are in their late fifties and early sixties in a set of years beginning in 1969 and ending in 2004, she concludes that Farber and others overstate the change in the direction of instability. The length of workers' longest jobs has changed very little for male workers who completed their careers during these decades. Yet she converges with Farber in seeing significant change in today's prime-age workers, whom she argues are indeed seeing a decline in long-tenure jobs. When she trains an eye on the period beginning in 1975 or 1980, the period that coincides with a sharp uptick in inequality, she too sees evidence of a decline in the longest tenure of jobs for men. As these younger cohorts replace their fathers and mothers, the more common experience for Americans will be shorter-term job tenure. But because the labor force is composed at present of men and women who are starting and ending their careers, the majority experience today (with average job tenure of twenty-two years) may not mirror the majorities of the future.

The pattern emerging in younger workers is a consequence of increasing international competition and the wave of corporate downsizing that began to take its toll on today's labor force in the 1980s, barely pausing for a breath as we crest into the second decade of this century. That globalization is at the root of the change is reinforced by Farber's finding that we see virtually no change in the job tenure picture in the public sector, where unions remain a fixture and lifetime employment is much closer to the norm. No wonder, then, that the nation's most vulnerable workers—inner-city minorities—dream of finding "city jobs."[7] Postal workers, transit workers, teachers, social workers, policemen, and firemen—these are the jobs that have been (relatively speaking) protected from the ravages of international competition and inner-city workers know them as the Holy Grail of the work world.

That goal is becoming ever harder for low-skilled and poorly educated workers, especially minority men, to lay their hands on. Benjamin J. Keys and Sheldon Danziger zero in on this population and ask how the general trends identified in Farber and Stevens have affected those at the bottom of the stratification system. This has been a dismal period for the nation's low-skilled workers by almost any measure. Real hourly wages are 9% below their 1979 levels for high school dropouts and are only 5% higher for high school graduates. The same trends that have impacted better-educated workers—declining rates of union representation, increased international competition, and skill-biased technological change—have hammered poorly educated workers.

How have these trends impacted job security for those at the bottom? Keys and Danziger note that these workers are not likely to see golden parachutes when they lose their jobs and will probably spend months rather than weeks seeking a new position. Because they begin with low wages, they may actually be less likely to experience downward mobility in terms of earnings, but this is little comfort. Drawing on the Panel Study of Income Dynamics, which permits the authors to focus on change over the last thirty-five years, Keys and Danziger show that younger, less-educated men are more likely to experience unemployment than their better-educated counterparts and once out of a job have found it harder to land new positions. Hence while the secular changes identified by Farber and Stevens matter over all, they impact particular demographic groups in the labor market differentially. In an economy that increasingly privileges education—not only for wages and occupational prestige, but for employment stability itself—the least qualified, most stigmatized workers are feeling the turmoil more than anyone else.

Does that mean that the subjective experience of insecurity has been most pronounced for them? Yes and no. Elisabeth Jacobs and Katherine S. Newman address this question by looking at who *worries* about job loss, financial stability, and reemployment. Consistent with the structural findings in the earlier chapters of this volume, "Rising Angst?" finds that lower-income, less-educated workers are indeed more concerned about their economic security than the more privileged members of the labor force. Workers accurately gauge their chances of losing a job, finding a new one, or remaining financially stable from year to year. Educated managers know that they can draw on their skills and experience to protect themselves, relative to those who have less to offer, when heads are rolling or unemployment rises. Yet those protections are not as strong as they once were and hence Jacobs and Newman's analysis of the General Social Survey shows that the most pronounced *change* in the direction of subjective insecurity is surfacing among the most advantaged workers.

On virtually every measure that matters, highly educated workers feel disadvantaged relative to the CEOs above them, who have seen their pay rise into the stratosphere and their stock options balloon. Relative to the titans of Wall Street, the average managerial worker feels vulnerable. Do they accept the widening inequality that has permitted the very top to pull so far away from the average worker, even the average manager? Does the American population think that government should play any role in reducing that gap? One might imagine that social norms support increasing evidence of inequality and look askance at government intervention that can dampen it. After all, from the late 1990s onward, the nation handed the Republican Party a long string of victories in presidential and congressional elections. Surely this suggests popular support for a laissez-faire perspective and the widening gaps in income and economic security that come with it.

GSS data suggest otherwise: Respondents are growing less tolerant of income inequality and are actually modestly more supportive of the role government plays in redistributing income from high- to low-earning Americans and from the rich to the poor. Jacobs and Newman point to National Election Studies data from 1992 to 2004 that reinforce this conclusion, as support for federal welfare spending reached a ten-year high in 2002. Perhaps the tolerance for inequality has reached its limits and a reaction is setting in, driven in part by the increasing insecurity that the most advantaged workers feel about their own futures (rather than their concern for the least advantaged, which has changed very little since the 1960s).

How do these sentiments figure in political preferences? And what do they portend for the electoral landscape? These are the central questions underlying Philipp Rehm's chapter, and he shows the connection is tight indeed. People who face high risks in the labor market tend to sympathize with the Democratic Party, while people who enjoy relative stability in employment favor the Republican perspective. Cross-pressures plague those groups in the middle, who are high income but vulnerable to job loss. Rehm shows that over time income and the risk of unemployment became increasingly related to each other, a trend he calls "risk polarization." Increasing income inequality and risk polarization should give the Democratic Party the upper hand. Yet as this trend has become clearer, the emergence of the "values agenda" has become more pronounced. This, Rehm argues, is no accident. Echoing the arguments of John Roemer[8] and Thomas Frank,[9] Rehm suggests that parties likely to lose on one set of issues (in this instance, economic security) have a strong incentive to change the subject (to abortion, crime, or foreign policy). And that is exactly what we have witnessed in political debate.

Ironically, Rehm points out, the increasingly tight association of income and risk polarization decreases the role that risk exposure plays in shaping political preferences. Once we know the income of an occupation, we are pretty sure about the risks of unemployment it incurs. These two features are not as independent of each other as they once were, a phenomenon that former GM workers know all too well. Their jobs have gone south and with that, the diversity of income and risk that once defined the blue-collar experience. In its place we see a divided nation, with the well to do and relatively well-insulated facing off against the less comfortable and more vulnerable.

Since 9/11, the nation has been riveted by the consequences of terrorism and the unfolding catastrophe of war in Iraq. All eyes have been turned overseas and away from the domestic scene. Yet there is a great deal of unfinished business at home and the election season of 2008, and the congressional elections that will follow in the future, have already kindled greater attention to the challenges we face in our own backyard. Among the most pressing for most American households is the question of labor market security, for on its back rides the prosperity and stability that underwrites the family and the prospects for succeeding generations. For the average worker, the abstractions we use to describe the dynamics of the labor market are far less meaningful than the paycheck he knows and the income she depends on. As these authors demonstrate, there is reason to worry for their futures, and they know it.

NOTES

1   Louis Uchitelle, "Jobless Rate Climbs to 5.7% as 51,000 Jobs are Lost in July," *New York Times*, August 2, 2008, http://www.nytimes.com/2008/08/02/business/02econ.html?scp=2&sq=unemployment&st=cse; Peter Goodman, "A Hidden Toll on Employment: Cut to Part Time," *New York Times*, July 31, 2008, http://www.nytimes.com/2008/07/31/business/economy/31jobs.html?scp=1&sq=part%20time%20work&st=cse.

2   Lawrence Mishel, Jared Bernstein, and Syliva Allegretto, *The State of Working America: 2006–2007* (Washington, DC: Economic Policy Institute, 2008), 227.

3   Elizabeth Warren and Amelia Tyagi, *The Two Income Trap* (New York: Basic Books, 2003).

4   Paul Osterman, *Getting Started: The Youth Labor Market* (Cambridge, MA: The MIT Press, 1980).

5   Paul Osterman, "Gains from Growth? The Impact of Full Employment in Boston on Poverty," in The *Urban Underclass*, ed. Christopher Jencks and Paul Peterson (Washington, DC: Brookings Institution Press, 1991), 122–34.

6   Katherine S. Newman, *No Shame in My Game: The Working Poor in the Inner City* (New York: Knopf, 1999); *Chutes and Ladders: Navigating the Low Wage Labor Market* (Cambridge, MA: Harvard University Press, 2006).

7   Newman, *No Shame in My Game*.

8   John Roemer, *Political Competition: Theory and Applications* (Cambridge, MA: Harvard University Press, 2001).

9   Thomas Frank, *What's the Matter with Kansas?: How Conservatives Won the Heart of America* (New York: Henry Holt, 2004).

CHAPTER ONE

Short(er) Shrift | *The Decline in Worker–Firm Attachment in the United States*

HENRY S. FARBER

Long-term employment relationships have long been an important feature of the labor market in the United States. However, increased international competition and the wave of corporate downsizing in the 1990s
raised concerns that such long-term employment relationships were
disappearing. To the extent that there has been a substantial change in
career employment dynamics, young workers who recently entered the
labor force or will in the future are going to face a very different type of
career than did earlier cohorts.

In this chapter, I examine evidence on job durations from 1973 to
2006 in order to determine the extent to which, in fact, the structure of
jobs, indicated by the likelihood of long-term employment, is changing.
I use data from twenty-one supplements to the Current Population Survey (CPS) over the 1973–2006 period that contain information on how
long workers have been employed by their current firm. These data allow
me to investigate how the career dynamics of workers has changed over
time. In particular, I examine various age-specific measures of the length
of employment relationships in order to determine whether workers are
experiencing a different level of job stability than workers of the same
age in earlier years.

The evolution of the structure of careers in the United States has played out in the context of dramatic growth in employment over the last forty years. Civilian employment was 85.1 million in 1973 and rose to 144.4 million in 2006.[1] Thus, almost sixty million jobs have been created on net in the past thirty-three years, for an average rate of employment growth of 1.6% per year over this period. Despite this record of sustained growth in employment in the United States, there is long-standing concern that the quality of the stock of jobs in the economy more generally is deteriorating. The concern about job quality is based in part on the fact that the share of employment that is in manufacturing has been declining over a long period of time.[2] This has led to the view that as high-quality manufacturing jobs are lost, perhaps to import competition, they are being replaced by low-quality service-sector jobs (so-called hamburger-flipping jobs). The high-quality jobs are characterized by relatively high wages, full-time employment, substantial fringe benefits, and, perhaps most importantly, substantial job security (low rates of turnover). The low-quality jobs are characterized disproportionately by relatively low wages, part-time employment, an absence of fringe benefits, and low job security (high rates of turnover).[3]

The results are clear-cut. By virtually any measure, males in the private sector have been with their current employers for less time at specific ages. Age-specific overall mean tenure has fallen substantially for these workers and particularly for those over forty years of age. In addition, men employed in the private sector have become much less likely to be in a long-term employment relationship. Mirroring this decline in tenure and long-term employment relationships, there has been an increase in "churning" (defined as the proportion of workers in jobs with less than one year of tenure) for males in the private sector as they enter their thirties and later. In contrast, women have seen no systematic change in job durations or the incidence of long-term employment relationships in the private sector.

Interestingly, there has been an *increase* in job durations and the incidence of long-term employment relationships in the public sector, with the increase more pronounced for women. The private–public contrast is informative because government employment has generally seen neither the increase in competitive pressures nor the decline in unionization (partly a result of increased competitive pressures) experienced in the private sector.[4]

I conclude that (1) the structure of jobs in the private sector has moved away from long-term relationships, (2) this decline has been offset for females by their increased attachment to the labor force, and (3) the public sector has been less susceptible to the competitive forces that are likely causing the changes in the private sector. It seems clear that more recent cohorts of workers are less likely than their parents to have a career characterized by a "lifetime" job with a single employer.

REVIEW OF RECENT LITERATURE ON JOB STABILITY

Several recent papers have used CPS data on job tenure to examine changes in employment stability. Kenneth Swinnerton and Howard Wial, working with data from 1979 through 1991, analyze job retention rates computed from artificial cohorts and conclude that there has been a secular decline in job stability in the 1980s.[5] In contrast, Francis X. Diebold, David Neumark, and Daniel Polsky, using CPS data on tenure from 1973 through 1991 to compute retention rates for artificial cohorts, find that aggregate retention rates were fairly stable over the 1980s but that retention rates declined for high school dropouts and for high school graduates relative to college graduates over this period.[6] I interpret a direct exchange between Diebold, Polsky, and Neumark and Swinnerton and Wial as supporting the view that the period from 1979 to 1991 is not a period of generally decreasing job stability.[7] Using CPS data on job tenure from 1973 through 1993, Farber determined that the prevalence of long-term employment has not declined over time but that the distribution of long jobs has shifted.[8] He finds that less-educated men are less likely to hold long jobs than they were previously but that this is offset by a substantial increase in the rate at which women hold long jobs. Farber examines CPS data on job tenure from 1979 through 1996, and finds that the prevalence of long-term employment relationships among men declined by 1996 to its lowest level since 1979.[9] In contrast, long-term employment relationships became somewhat more common among women.

Stephen J. Rose uses data from the Panel Study of Income Dynamics (PSID) to measure job stability by examining the fraction of male workers who do not report any job changes in a given time period, typically ten years.[10] Rose finds that the fraction of workers who reported no job changes in a given length of time was higher in the 1970s than in the 1980s. He argues that this is evidence of increasing instability of employment.

The Russell Sage Foundation sponsored a conference organized by David Neumark on "Changes in Job Stability and Job Security" in 1998.[11] The evidence presented here is mixed regarding whether job tenure was declining. David A. Jaeger and Ann Huff Stevens use data from the PSID and the CPS mobility and benefit supplements on (roughly) annual rates of job change to try to reconcile evidence from the CPS and PSID on job stability.[12] They find no change in the share of males in short jobs and some decline between the late 1980s and mid-1990s in the share of males with at least ten years of tenure.[13] David Neumark, Daniel Polsky, and Daniel Hansen find a similar decline in long-term employment but conclude that this does not reflect a secular trend.[14] Peter Gottschalk and Robert Moffitt use monthly data from the Survey of Income and Program Participation (SIPP), along with annual data from the SIPP and the PSID, and they see no evidence of an upward trend in job insecurity in the 1980s and 1990s.[15] Robert Valletta uses data from the PSID from 1976 to 1993 and finds some decline in long-term employment relationships.[16]

In more recent work, Jay Stewart works with data from the March CPS to investigate two aspects of job security.[17] The first, the likelihood of leaving a job, shows no particular trend from 1975 through 2000 based on these data. The second, the likelihood of making an employment-to-employment transition, increased over this period, while the likelihood of making an employment-to-unemployment transition decreased. Stewart concludes that the cost of changing jobs has decreased.

Ann Huff Stevens examines data from several longitudinal histories of older male workers (late fifties and early sixties) with regard to changes over time in the length of longest job held during careers.[18] She finds that there has been no change between the late 1960s and early 2000s and concludes that there has not been a decline in the incidence of "lifetime jobs." A careful reading of her results shows an increase in average longest tenure from about 22 years among older workers in 1969 to 24 years in 1980 followed by a decline to 21.4 years in 2002. A reasonable interpretation of this pattern is that the earliest cohorts had jobs interrupted by service in World War II, resulting in lower average longest tenure than subsequent cohorts. The decline since 1980 may then reflect a real decline in job durations. Additionally, the most recent cohort examined by Stevens was born in the 1940s, so her analysis cannot shed light on the experience of more recent birth cohorts.

In a recent paper, I present an analysis of the same data I use here organized around an examination of the experience of different birth cohorts, although I make no distinction between the public and private sectors.[19] I conclude that more recent birth cohorts of men have experienced a sharp reduction in job tenure and the incidence of long-term employment relationships.

A careful reading of this earlier literature does not yield a clear answer regarding changes in the incidence of long-term employment relationships. I turn now to my analysis, which covers a long time period in a consistent way, in order to determine what, in fact, has happened to long-term employment relationships in the United States.

MEASURING THE CHANGE IN TENURE OVER TIME

My analysis relies on a sample consisting of not self-employed workers aged twenty to sixty-four from the twenty-one CPS supplements covering the period from 1973 to 2006. The sample contains 876,063 workers, and the data are described in more detail in the Appendix.

I organize my analysis of changes over time in the distribution of job durations by examining age-specific values of various distributional measures of job tenure in different years. No one statistic can completely characterize a distribution, and I focus on several measures here:

- Mean job tenure (years with the current employer). Note that this is not mean completed job duration since the jobs sampled are still in progress.
- The age-specific probability that workers report being on their job at least ten years. Because younger workers cannot have accumulated substantial job tenure, I restrict this analysis to workers at least thirty-five years of age, and I examine how these probabilities have evolved over time. This allows me to investigate changes in the transition from the early "job-shopping" phase of a career to more stable longer-term employment relationships in mid-career.

- The age-specific probability that workers report being in their job at least twenty years. Because younger workers cannot have accumulated substantial job tenure, I restrict this analysis to workers forty-five years of age and older, and I examine how these probabilities have evolved over time. This allows me to investigate changes in the incidence of longer-term employment relationship later in careers.
- The age-specific probability that workers report holding their jobs for less than one year. This provides another approach to investigating changes in the transition from the early job-shopping phase of a career to more stable longer-term employment relationships.

An important measurement issue is related to cyclical changes in the composition of the sample. It is clear that workers with little seniority are more likely than high-tenure workers to lose their jobs in downturns.[20] Thus, we would expect that the incidence of long-term important employment, as measured by the fraction of workers with tenure exceeding some threshold, to be countercyclical. Tight labor markets will lead the distribution of job durations to lie to the left of the distribution in slack labor markets. These cyclical influences need to be kept in mind when interpreting the results.

THE EVOLUTION OF JOB TENURE

MEAN TENURE

Figure 1.1 contains separate plots of mean tenure for males by age for three time periods covered by the data (1973–83, 1984–95, 1996–2006).[21] These show clearly that mean tenure is rising with age in both the public and private sectors. With regard to shifts over time in the tenure distribution, age-specific mean tenure for males employed in the private sector has declined substantially, particularly for older workers. For example, mean tenure for males at age fifty in the private sector declined from 13.5 years in the 1973–83 period to 11.4 years in the 1996–2006 period. The pattern in the public sector is the opposite. For example, mean tenure for males at age fifty in the public sector *increased* from 13.6 years in the 1973–83 period to 16.1 years in the 1996–2006 period.

Figure 1.2 contains the same plots for females, and the pattern in the private sector is quite different than that for males. While mean tenure

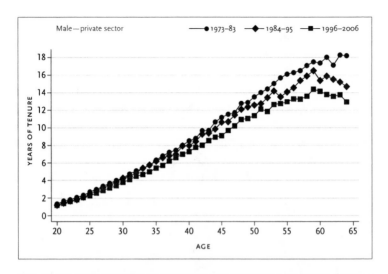

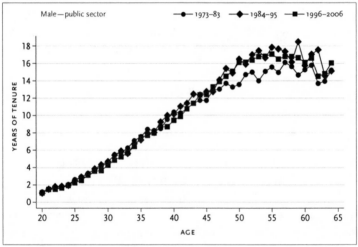

Figure 1.1   Mean tenure for males, by age and year

for females is increasing with age, tenure levels are substantially lower than those for males in the private sector. Importantly, there appears to have been no change in age-specific job tenure for females employed in the private sector. This is despite the well-documented increase in female attachment to the labor force. In contrast, females in the public

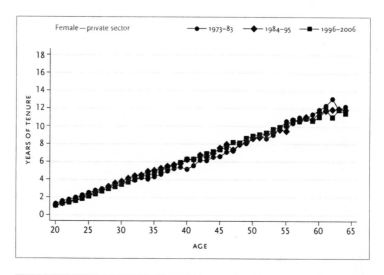

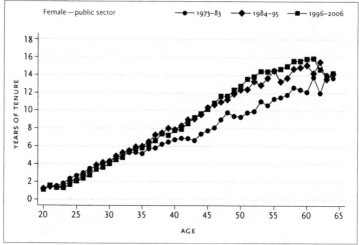

Figure 1.2   Mean tenure for females, by age and year

sector have seen a substantial increase in mean job tenure. For example, mean tenure for females at age fifty in the public sector increased from 9.3 years in the 1973–83 period to 12.8 years in the 1996–2006 period. One explanation for this pattern may be that the economy-wide changes that drove the increase in female labor force attachment in the last thirty

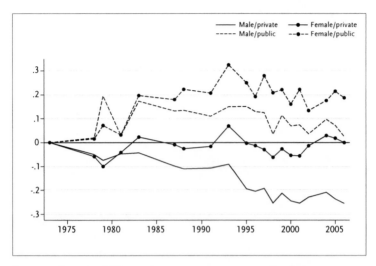

Figure 1.3 Proportional difference from 1973, mean tenure, controlling for age

years have been offset in the private sector by the same forces that have led to the decline in male tenure in the private sector.

Another approach to summarizing the data is to estimate a linear model of the natural logarithm of tenure of the form

$$ln(T_{ijt}) = Y_t + A_j + \varepsilon_{ijt} \ (1)$$

where T_{ijt} is tenure in years for individual i at age j in year t, Y_t is a calendar year indicator, and A_j is a years-of-age indicator. This logarithmic specification embodies the plausible implicit assumption that proportional year effects on mean tenure are constant across ages and, equivalently, that the proportional age effects on mean tenure are constant across years.[22] A more detailed investigation would allow for year effects that vary by age since changes in job security could express themselves differentially at various ages. However, the model in equation 1 fits the data quite well, and it serves as a good summary of the data.[23]

I estimate the model in equation 1 separately for men and women in the public and private sectors using ordinary least squares (OLS), weighted by the CPS final sample weights. The implied proportional differences from the 1973 value of age-specific mean tenure are plotted in figure 1.3.[24]

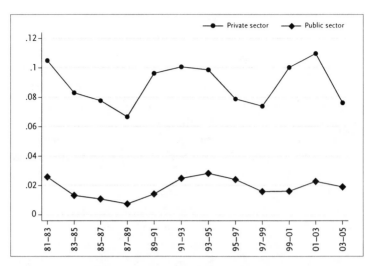

Figure 1.4 Three-year job loss rates, by sector of employment

The patterns are quite different for the four groups of workers. There is a sharp decline of about 25% in age-specific mean tenure for male private-sector workers between the 1973 and 2006. In contrast, there is no systematic change over time in age-specific mean tenure for female private-sector workers. The public sector shows a dramatic increase in age-specific mean tenure both for men and for women over the sample period. Tenure for males in the public sector increased by about 18% between 1973 and 1983 before declining somewhat by 2006 to approximately the 1973 level. Age-specific mean tenure for females in the public sector was 30% higher in the early 1990s than in 1973 and remained about 20% higher in 2006 then it was in 1973.

These patterns are consistent with those found in figures 1.1 and 1.2. They suggest a decline in long-term employment opportunities in the private sector that is most evident for males and is offset to some extent for females by their increased attachment to the labor force.

The increase in mean tenure in the public sector could reflect an increase in the relative attractiveness of public-sector jobs that is magnified for females by their increased attachment to the labor force. Indeed job security appears to be higher in public-sector jobs. Figure 1.4 contains plots of three-year job loss rates calculated from the Displaced

Workers Surveys (DWS), available biannually from 1984–2006.[25] The rate of job loss in the public sector is approximately one-fourth of the private-sector rate, and it exhibits less cyclical sensitivity. To the extent that private-sector jobs have become less secure, it may be the case that public-sector jobs have become relatively more attractive. The resulting lower quit rates from public-sector jobs would serve to reinforce the already high job tenure evident in that sector.

In addition to the increased presence of women in the labor force, there are other important changes that could be related to the decline in tenure. First is the well-known large increase in average educational attainment during the twentieth century. While there is not a clear relationship between educational attainment and tenure, I account for education levels in my investigation of the decline in mean job tenure.[26] Second, and potentially more important, is the substantial increase in the immigrant share of the U.S. labor force. By definition, newly arrived immigrants cannot have substantial tenure. Data on immigration are not available in any CPS with tenure data prior to 1995. Analysis of the data since 1995 illustrates both the sharp increase in immigrant share in the labor force and the fact that immigrants have lower job tenure than natives. The weighted immigrant fraction of the labor force in my sample increased steadily from 9.45% in 1995 to 14.7% in 2006. On average between 1995 and 2006, immigrant workers had 2.14 years lower tenure than natives (s.e. = 0.034). Immigrant workers were only slightly younger than natives over the same period (average difference = 0.98 years [s.e. = 0.050]).[27]

An important question is how much of the decline in observed tenure since 1973 is due to the increased immigrant presence in the labor force. While not directly observable prior to 1995, immigrant status is strongly correlated with race and Hispanic ethnicity, which is observed in all years. My tabulations of the CPS from 1995 to 2006 show that immigrants are highly concentrated among nonwhites and Hispanics. Only 3.6% of white non-Hispanics are immigrants, while over 50% of Hispanics (white and nonwhite) are immigrants. Additionally, a growing fraction of nonwhite non-Hispanics are immigrants, rising from 18.7% in 1995 to 28.2% in 2006. The rising overall immigrant share over this period is reflected in the growing share of Hispanics and nonwhites in the labor force. The Hispanic share of employment in my sample increased from

9.0% in 1995 to 13.4% in 2006 and the nonwhite share of employment increased from 15.2% to 17.2% over the same period. Another perspective on the same facts is that 75% to 80% of immigrant workers in the United States between 1995 and 2006 are either Hispanic or nonwhite.

In order to account, at least partly, for the role of increased immigration in the decline in tenure, I estimate age-specific proportional differences in mean tenure relative to 1973 controlling for race, Hispanic ethnicity, and their interaction, as well as age and education. I estimate

$$ln(T_{ijt}) = \alpha_1 NW_i + \alpha_2 H_i + \alpha_3 H_i NW_i + ED_i\gamma + Y_t + A_j + \varepsilon_{ijt}, \; (2)$$

where NW_i is an indicator for nonwhite, H_i is an indicator for Hispanic ethnicity, and ED_i is a vector of indicators for four educational categories. In parallel with figure 1.3, figure 1.5 contains separate plots for males and females in the private and public sectors of the proportional differences from 1973 in mean tenure based on equation 2. The time-series patterns controlling for age, education, race, and Hispanic ethnicity are similar to those controlling for age alone. The additional controls account for about 20% of the decline evident in figure 1.3.

There remains a sharp decline of about 20% in age-specific mean tenure for male private-sector workers between the 1973 and 2006, and there is still no systematic change over time in age-specific mean tenure for female private-sector workers. The public sector continues to show an increase in age-specific mean tenure both for men and for women over the sample period. Tenure for males in the private sector increased by about 18% between 1973 and 1983 before declining somewhat by 2006 to approximately the 1973 level. Age-specific mean tenure for females in the public sector was 30% higher in the early 1990s than in 1973 and remained about 15% higher in 2006 then it was in 1973.

It is clear from the analysis in this subsection that age-specific mean tenure has declined dramatically over time and that only about 20% of this decline can be accounted for by the sharp growth in immigrants in the labor market. This decline is concentrated among men in the private sector. Mean tenure increased for both men and women in the public sector.

LONG-TERM EMPLOYMENT

Long-term employment is common in the U.S. labor market. I consider two measures:

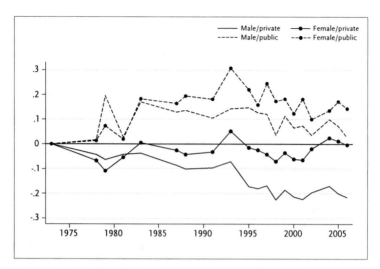

Figure 1.5 Proportional difference from 1973, mean tenure, controlling for age, education, race, and hispanic ethnicity

- the fraction of workers aged thirty-five to sixty-four who have been with their employer at least ten years (the "ten-year rate"), and
- the fraction of workers aged forty-five to sixty-four who have been with their employer at least twenty years (the "twenty-year rate").

Figure 1.6 contains plots of these two measures over the 1973–2006 period for men and women in the public and private sectors. It is clear that the incidence of long-term employment has declined dramatically for men in the private sector, with the ten-year rate falling from about 50% to about 35% and the twenty-year rate falling from about 35% to about 20% between 1973 and 2006. In contrast, the incidence of long-term employment for men in the public sector increased over the same period, with the ten-year rate increasing from 50% to 60% in 2000 before falling to 55% in 2006. Over the same period the twenty-year rate for men employed in the public sector increased from 25% in 1973 to 40% in 1990 before falling off to 35% by 2006.

The incidence of long-term employment among women in the private sector remained steady between 1973 and 2006, at a ten-year rate of about 30% and a twenty-year rate of about 15%. In sharp contrast, the incidence of long-term employment among women in the public sector

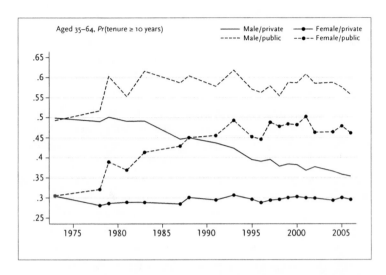

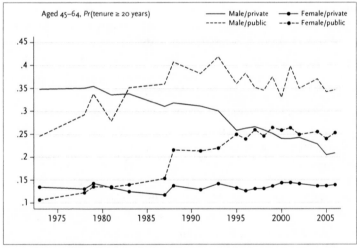

Figure 1.6 Fraction of workers in long-term jobs, by year

increased substantially, with the ten-year rate increasing from 30% in 1973 to 45% in 2006 and the twenty-year rate increasing from 10% to 25% over the same period.

Because these measures are sensitive to the age distribution and other observable characteristics, I estimate age-specific year effects using the same approach I used for mean tenure. I estimate linear probability models using the same specification of explanatory variables (year, age, education, race, Hispanic ethnicity, and the interaction of race and Hispanic ethnicity) in equation 2, and I report the estimated year effects (differences from 1973) from this analysis in figure 1.7.

Figure 1.7 contains separate plots for males and females by sector of employment of the year effects (1973=0) for the ten-year rate (top panel) and the twenty-year rate (bottom panel). The age-specific probability that a male worker in the private sector has been with his employer for at least ten years decreased steadily by about ten percentage points. A decline of the same magnitude is also found for the twenty-year rate for private-sector male workers. These ten-percentage-point declines are substantial given the 1973 base ten-year rate of 50% and the base twenty-year rate of 35% (figure 1.6). The rates of long-term employment for females in the private sector show no change between 1973 and 2006.

As with the simple means in figure 1.6, the long-term employment rates for both men and women in the public sector have increased since 1973. The increase has been particularly sharp for women, with both the ten- and twenty-year rates increasing by more than ten percentage points (from a 1973 base of 30% and 10%, respectively).

Taken together, the analysis of the changes in average tenure (figure 1.5) and in the likelihood of long-term employment (figure 1.7) across cohorts shows clearly that average tenure has declined and long-term employment has become much less common for males in the private sector. Among females in the private sector, average tenure and the incidence of long-term employment have remained steady. Workers in the public sector, on the other hand, have seen an increase in both average tenure and the incidence of long-term employment.

The private- public-sector contrast may reflect an increase in the relative attractiveness of stable public-sector jobs that reduces voluntary job changes as well as the lower reported job-loss rate in public-sector jobs (figure 1.4).

The difference in patterns between males and females in the private sector likely reflects the common factors reducing tenure for all workers offset for females by their dramatically increased attachment to the labor force over the past half century. This increase in attachment is also

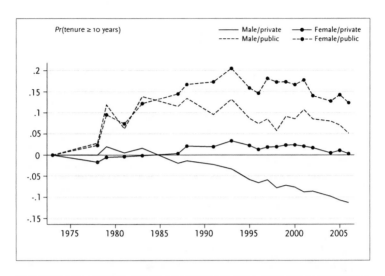

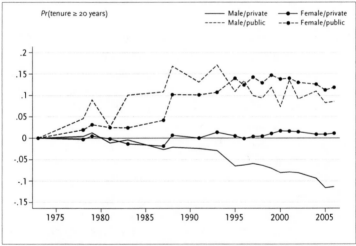

Figure 1.7 Difference from 1973 in the probability of long-term employment, controlling for age, education, race, and hispanic ethnicity

reflected in the larger increase in tenure and long-term employment among women relative to men in the public sector.

A key conclusion is that the structure of employment in the private sector in the United States has become less oriented toward long-term jobs. Since public-sector employment as a fraction of total employment

	MALE / PRIVATE	FEMALE / PRIVATE	MALE / PUBLIC	FEMALE / PUBLIC	ALL
AGE 20–29	0.340	0.373	0.281	0.314	0.349
AGE 30–39	0.174	0.218	0.090	0.148	0.181
AGE 40–49	0.122	0.156	0.056	0.085	0.124
AGE 50–59	0.094	0.113	0.043	0.053	0.090
AGE 60–64	0.080	0.090	0.052	0.042	0.077
ALL	0.190	0.224	0.100	0.134	0.190

The new job rate is the fraction of workers reporting less than one year of tenure with their current employer. Based on data for not self-employed workers 20–64 years of age from nineteen CPSs covering the period from 1973 to 2006. Weighted by CPS final sample weights. N=876,063.

Table 1.1   New job rate, by gender and sector of employment, 1973–2005

has remained steady at about 18% to 20% and seems unlikely to increase, it appears that young workers today will be less likely than their parents to have a "lifetime" job.

CHURNING: ARE THERE MORE VERY SHORT JOBS?

The opposite but related pole of the job tenure distribution is short-term jobs. I have presented evidence that half of all new jobs (worker–employer matches) end within the first year.[28] As I show below, a substantial fraction (around 20%) of all jobs have current tenure less than one year ("new jobs"). Not surprisingly, young workers are more likely than older workers to be in new jobs. High rates of job change among young workers are a natural result of search for a good job or a good match.[29]

Table 1.1 contains the new-job rate by ten-year age group for males and females by sector of employment. This illustrates the sharp decline in the new-job rate as workers age through their twenties especially and into their thirties. This decline is sharper for males, and the new-job rate is slightly higher for females in all age groups. This reflects the fact that females are more likely to leave and reenter the labor force in mid-career.

In order to investigate how the new-job rate has changed over time, figure 1.8 contains plots of the new-job rate by year for each of the four sex/sector groups. The new-job rate increased for males employed in the private sector and decreased for females employed in the public sector. There was a small decline in the new-job rate for males employed in the public sector and no change for females in the private sector.

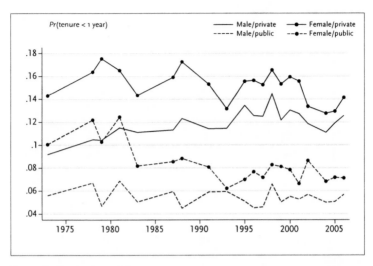

Figure 1.8 Fraction in new jobs

In order to account for differences by age and other characteristics, I estimate age-specific year effects using the same approach I used for means and for the probability of long-term employment. I estimate linear probability models of the probability of being in a new job using the same specification of explanatory variables (year, age, education, race, Hispanic ethnicity) in equation 2. Figure 1.9 contains separate plots for males and females of the difference by year in the new-job rate relative to 1973.

The age-specific probability that a male worker in the private sector has been with his employer for less than one year increased by about three percentage points between the 1973 and 2006. Once again, there is no systematic change for females in the private sector. Nor is there any change for males employed in the private sector. However, there is a two-percentage-point decline in the age-specific new-job rate for females in the public sector.

The decline in the new-job rate by age evident in table 1 raises two interesting questions regarding the decline in mean tenure and long-term employment and how this decline is related to the rate of "churning" in the labor market:

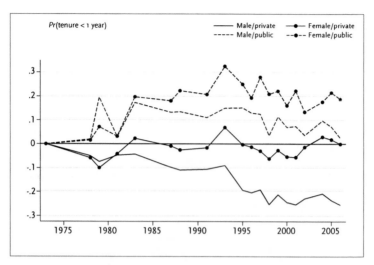

Figure 1.9 Difference from 1973 in the new-job probability, controlling for age, education, race, and hispanic ethnicity

1. Are young workers taking longer to find good (long-lasting) matches or jobs? This would imply an increase in the new-job rate among younger workers.
2. Are older workers having more difficulty finding good matches when they lose jobs that may formerly have been "lifetime" jobs? This would imply an increase in the new-job rate among older workers.

An implicit constraint in the model I use to estimate the changes (based on equation 2) presented in figure 1.9 is that the changes over time are constant across age groups. Given the role that job change plays in matching and job search early in careers, I estimate separate year effects for different age groups. The top panel of figure 1.10 contains differences by year in the new-job rate relative to 1973 estimated using a sample of workers aged twenty to twenty-nine. These estimates, which vary quite a bit year to year, show no secular pattern but a strong cyclical pattern. The new-job rate is higher in strong economic times as employers increase hiring and lower in weaker times as workers are less likely to quit to take new jobs.

The bottom panel of figure 1.10 contains differences by year in the new-job rate relative to 1973 estimated using a sample of workers aged

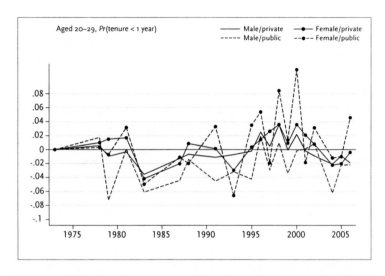

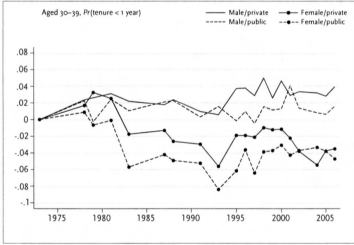

Figure 1.10 Difference from 1973 in the new-job probability, controlling for age, education, race, and hispanic ethnicity

thirty to thirty-nine. These estimated year effects differ substantially from those for workers in their twenties. There is an increase of about 4 percentage points in the new-job rate for males in their thirties in the private sector and a decrease of about 4 percentage points for females in their thirties in both sectors between 1973 and 2006. The pattern for males is consistent with the hypothesis that men are job shopping in their twenties and have become less likely to settle into longer-term jobs in their thirties. The pattern for females, which is stronger in the public sector, likely reflects an increase in attachment to the labor force by women as they enter their thirties.

Given that older workers are less likely to be in long-term jobs, I next investigate how the new-job rate has changed for workers aged forty and older. The top panel of figure 1.11 contains differences by year in the new-job rate relative to 1973 estimated using a sample of workers aged forty to forty-nine. The bottom panel of this figure contains differences by year in the new-job rate relative to 1973 using a sample of workers aged fifty to sixty-four. Both plots show an increase in the probability of being in a new job for males employed in the private sector. The magnitude of the increase (about two percentage points) is substantial when compared to the overall mean new-job rates for older men in table 1.1. The new-job rate for women in the public sector in their forties is decreased substantially, but the change is not reflected in the experience of women fifty and older.

The overall time-series pattern of the age-specific new-job rate is a general increase over time for men aged thirty and older. Part of this reflects an extension of the period of "job shopping" early in careers and part reflects increased probabilities of jobs ending later in careers. There is not much change over time in the age-specific new-job rate for women in either the public or private sectors aside from a substantial decline for women in their thirties, likely reflecting a reduced likelihood of withdrawing from and subsequently reentering the labor force in their thirties.

The overall pattern of results regarding mean job tenure and the incidence of long-term employment relationships suggests that there has been a substantial decline in long-term employment opportunities and a concomitant reduction in job security in the private sector. This is manifested directly in the reduction in job tenure and incidence of long-term employment relationships for men in the private sector. The fact that there is no such reduction for women in the private sector is likely a result of an offsetting increase in attachment of women to the labor force and to their jobs.

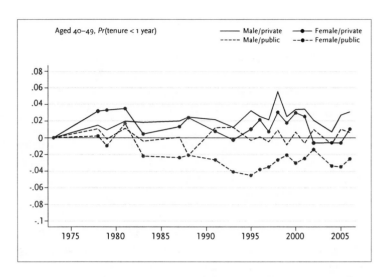

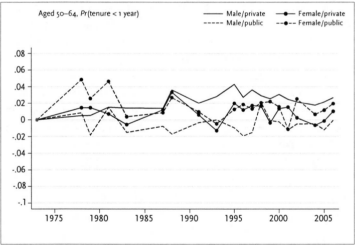

Figure 1.11   Difference from 1973 in the new-job probability, controlling for age, education, race, and hispanic ethnicity

Workers in the public sector have a very different experience. Job tenure and the incidence of long-term employment relationships have increased in the public sector for both men and women. The contrast in the experience of the private and public sectors reflects important differences between these sectors. There has not been the increase in competitive pressures or decline in unionization in the public sector that has been seen in the private sector and likely are important components of the decline in job security in the private sector. The fact that job tenure and the incidence of long-term employment relationships in the public sector grew more for women than for men is consistent with the stability of the public sector reinforced for women by their increased attachment to the labor force.

Further analysis of churning in the labor market as reflected in the new-job rate (the fraction of jobs with tenure less than one year) indicates that there has consistently been a high level of turnover for young workers (less than thirty years of age), both male and female. However, as these workers age into their thirties, it appears that males have become less likely to settle into longer-term jobs as reflected by an increase in the new-job rate for males in this age group. In contrast, females in their thirties have become more likely to stay in their jobs.

I conclude that the nature of the private-sector employment relationship in the United States has changed substantially in ways that make jobs less secure and workers more mobile. The precise reasons for the changes in the structure of jobs that has yielded these changes are unclear and beg further research. One possibility is that the move away from long-term employment relationships reflects less demand by employers for a stable labor force, perhaps due to increased competitive pressure. What is clear is that young workers today should not look forward to the same type of career with one firm experienced by their parents.

APPENDIX: THE CPS DATA ON EMPLOYER TENURE

At irregular intervals, the Census Bureau has appended mobility supplements to the January or February Current Population Surveys. The years in which they did so include 1951, 1963, 1966, 1968, 1973, 1978, 1981, 1983, 1987, 1991, and the even years from 1996 to 2006. These supplements contain information on how long workers have been continuously employed by their current employer, and the questions are asked of all eight CPS rotation groups. However, only the supplements since 1973 are available in machine-readable form. Information on job durations is also available in pension and benefit supplements to the CPS in May of 1979, 1981, 1983, and 1988, and in April 1993. These supplements contain information on how long workers have been working for their current employer, and the questions are asked of four of the eight CPS rotation groups. Finally, information on job durations is available in the continuous and alternative employment arrangement supplements (CAEAS) to the CPS in February of 1995, 1997, 1999, 2001, and 2005. In total there are twenty-one CPS supplements with information on employer tenure available in machine-readable form over the period from 1973 to 2006, and my analysis relies on these data.[30]

With the exception of jobs of less than one year, all of the supplements before the February 1996 mobility supplement collect data on job duration in integer form reporting the number of years employed. For jobs of less than one year, the mobility supplements report the number of months employed while the pension and benefit supplements report only the fact that the job was less than one year old. The February 1996 and later mobility supplement ask workers how long they have worked continuously for their current employer and accepts a numerical response where the worker specifies the time units. The 1995–2005 CAEAS ask workers how long they have worked for their current employer and accepts a numerical response where the worker specifies the time units. Virtually all workers in jobs even five years old and all workers in jobs ten years old or longer report job durations in years.

One reasonable interpretation of the integer report of the number of years is that workers round to the nearest integer when they report jobs of duration of at least one year. (This ignores the heaping of the tenure distribution at multiples of five and ten years.) For example, a response of 10 years would imply tenure greater than or equal to 9.5 years and less than 10.5 years. In order to create a smooth tenure variable, I assume that the distribution of job tenure is uniform in these one-year intervals. Given a reported tenure of T years, I replace T by T − 0.5 + u, where u is a random variable distributed uniformly on the unit interval.[31]

My sample consists of 876,063 not self-employed workers aged twenty to sixty-four from the twenty-one CPS supplements covering the period from 1973 to 2006. The self-employed are not included because the concept of employer tenure is less clear for the self-employed, and, in any case, the CPS supplements do not contain consistent information on tenure for the self-employed.

NOTES

1   These statistics are taken from U.S. Bureau of Labor Statistics Series ID LNU02000000. This is the civilian employment level derived from the Current Population Survey for workers aged sixteen and older.

2   The manufacturing share of nonfarm employment has been falling for over fifty years. Manufacturing's share was 30.9% in 1950 and fell to 10.4% in 2006. These statistics are taken from U.S. Bureau of Labor Statistics Series ID CEU00000001 and CEU30000001 derived from the Current Employment Statistics payroll data.

3   For discussions of the quality of new and part-time jobs, see Henry S. Farber, "Job Creation in the United States: Good Jobs or Bad?" (Working Paper No. 385, Industrial Relations Section, Princeton University, July 1997); and Henry S. Farber and Helen Levy, "Recent Trends in Employer-Sponsored Health Insurance Coverage: Are Bad Jobs Getting Worse?" *Journal of Health Economics* (January 2000): 93–119.

4   For a discussion of the decline of unions in the private sector and the contrast with the public sector, see Henry S. Farber, "Union Membership in the United States: The Divergence between the Public and Private Sectors," in *Collective Bargaining in Education: Negotiating Change in Today's Schools,* ed. Jane Hannaway and Andrew J. Rotherham (Cambridge, MA: Harvard Education Press, 2006).

5   Kenneth Swinnerton and Howard Wial, "Is Job Stability Declining in the U.S. Economy?" *Industrial and Labor Relations Review* 48 (January 1995): 293–304.

6   Francis X. Diebold, David Neumark, and Daniel Polsky, "Job Stability in the United States," Working Paper No. 4859 (National Bureau of Economic Research, September 1994).

7   Francis X. Diebold, David Neumark, and Daniel Polsky, "Comment of Kenneth A.

Swinnerton and Howard Wial, 'Is Job Stability Declining in the U.S. Economy?'"
Industrial and Labor Relations Review 49 (January 1996): 348–52; Kenneth Swinnerton and Howard Wial, "Is Job Stability Declining in the U.S. Economy? Reply to
Diebold, Neumark, and Polsky," *Industrial and Labor Relations Review* 49 (January
1996): 352–55.

8   Henry S. Farber, "Are Lifetime Jobs Disappearing? Job Duration in the United
    States, 1973–93," in *Labor Statistics Measurement Issues*, ed. John Haltiwanger,
    Marilyn E. Manser, and Robert Topel (Chicago: University of Chicago Press, 1998),
    157–203.

9   Henry S. Farber, "Trends in Long-Term Employment in the United States: 1979–
    1996," in *Global Competition and the American Employment Landscape As We Enter
    the 21st Century: Proceedings of New York University 52d Annual Conference on Labor*,
    ed. Samuel Estreicher (New York: Kluwer Law International, 2000), 63–98.

10 Stephen J. Rose, "Declining Job Security and the Professionalization of Opportu-
    nity," Research Report 95-04 (National Commission for Employment Policy, April
    1995).

11 The proceedings of this conference are published in David Neumark, ed., *On the
    Job: Is Long-Term Employment a Thing of the Past?* (New York: Russell Sage Founda-
    tion, 2000), and a number of the papers are published in pt. 2, *Journal of Labor
    Economics* 17, no. 4 (October 1999).

12 David A. Jaeger and Ann Huff Stevens, "Is Job Stability in the United States Fall-
    ing? Reconciling Trends in the Current Population Survey and Panel Study of
    Income Dynamics," pt. 2, *Journal of Labor Economics* 17, no. 4 (October 1999):
    s1–s28.

13 Unfortunately, due to the design of the PSID, neither of these studies examines the
    mobility experience of women.

14 David Neumark, Daniel Polsky, and Daniel Hansen, "Has Job Stability Declined
    Yet? New Evidence for the 1990s," pt. 2, *Journal of Labor Economics* 17, no. 4 (Octo-
    ber 1999): s29–s64.

15 Peter Gottschalk and Robert Moffitt, "Changes in Job Instability and Insecurity
    Using Monthly Survey Data," pt. 2, *Journal of Labor Economics* 17, no. 4 (October
    1999): s91–s126.

16 Robert Valletta, "Declining Job Security," pt. 2, *Journal of Labor Economics* 17, no. 4
    (October 1999): s170–s197.

17 Jay Stewart. "Recent Trends in Job Stability and Job Security: Evidence from the
    March CPS," Working Paper No. 356 (Bureau of Labor Statistics, March 2002), 23.

18 Ann Huff Stevens, "The More Things Change the More They Stay the Same:

Trends in Long-Term Employment in the United States, 1969–2002," NBER Working Paper No. 11878 (December 2005).

19 Henry S. Farber, "Is the Company Man an Anachronism? Trends in Long-Term Employment in the U.S.," in *The Price of Independence: The Economics of Early Adulthood*, ed. Sheldon Danziger and Cecilia Rouse (New York: Russell Sage Foundation, 2007).

20 Katharine G. Abraham and James L. Medoff, "Length of Service and Layoffs in Union and Nonunion Work Groups," *Industrial and Labor Relations Review* 38 (October 1984): 87–97.

21 Means are calculated weighted by CPS final sample weights.

22 I do not estimate this model using absolute tenure because the implicit assumption in that case would be that absolute year effects on mean tenure are constant across ages and, equivalently, that absolute age effects on mean tenure are constant across years. This is clearly not plausible on inspection of figures 1 and 2, which demonstrate the fact that younger workers have very low levels of tenure.

23 I computed (separately for each of the four groups defined by sex and sector of employment) weighted mean tenure for each age/year combination and regressed these measures on a complete set of age and year fixed effects. This is essentially the main-effects model in equation 1 aggregated to the cell level. The R-squareds from these regressions are all in excess of 0.95.

24 The estimated year effects on mean tenure from equation 1, normalized to zero in 1973, are converted to proportional differences in mean tenure relative to 1973 as $exp(Y_t - Y_{1973}) - 1$.

25 The Displaced Worker Survey is a regular supplement to the Current Population Survey. Respondents are asked if they have lost a job in the three calendar years prior to the survey. Those who have lost jobs due to slack work, a plant closing, or a position being eliminated are asked a set of follow-up questions regarding the lost job and their experience since the job loss. I calculate job loss rates of these workers by dividing the number of workers who report such a job loss by sectoral employment as of the survey date. For a more detailed discussion of these data and issues of interpretation, see Henry S. Farber, "Job Loss and the Decline in Job Security in the United States," Working Paper No. 520 (Industrial Relations Section, Princeton University, September 2007).

26 Mean tenure in my analysis sample for each of four educational categories are ED<12: 7.3 years, ED=12: 7.3 years, ED 13–15: 6.4 years, and ED≥16: 7.3 years.

27 For a detailed analysis of the change in job tenure since 1995 that controls directly for immigrant status, see Farber, "Is the Company Man an Anachronism?"

28 Henry S. Farber, "The Analysis of Inter-Firm Worker Mobility," *Journal of Labor Economics* (October 1994): 554–93; "Mobility and Stability: The Dynamics of Job Change in Labor Markets," in *The Handbook of Labor Economics*, vol. 3B, ed. Orley Ashenfelter and Richard Layard (New York: North Holland Publishing Company, 1999), 2439–84.

29 A model of job search with this implication is presented by Kenneth Burdett, "Employee Search and Quits," *American Economic Review* 68 (1978): 212–20. A model of matching in the labor market with the same implication is offered by Boyan Jovanovic, "Job Matching and the Theory of Turnover," *Journal of Political Economics* 87 (1979): 972–90.

30 For a discussion of issues of comparability over time in these data, see the Appendix to Farber, "Is the Company Man an Anachronism?"

31 Where reported tenure is zero years, I assume that tenure is uniformly distributed between zero and one and define tenure as u. Given that jobs are more likely to end earlier in the first year than later in the first year, this is not completely accurate (see Farber, "Analysis of Inter-Firm Worker Mobility"). However, the measures used in my analysis will not be affected by this representation. Where reported tenure is exactly one year, I assume that true tenure is uniformly distributed between 1 and 1.5 and define tenure as $1 + u/2$.

CHAPTER TWO

Not So Fast | *Long-Term Employment in the United States, 1969–2004*

ANN HUFF STEVENS

In recent years, a conventional wisdom has emerged suggesting that the extent to which U.S. workers and employers form long-term relationships has significantly deteriorated. A 2003 *New York Times* article asserted that "workers today face a workplace that operates without the myth of job security."[1] A similar article from 2005 quotes the chief economist of a Chicago financial services firm as saying that the 1990s brought about major changes in our economy and, "It's no longer lifetime employment like it was thirty years ago."[2] When asked directly, workers themselves appear to be more worried than in previous years about the risk of separating from their employers.[3] Despite this widespread perception of major changes in the employment relationship in the United States, quantitative studies have, until very recently, shown little evidence of fundamental changes in empirical measures of job stability.

This chapter presents direct empirical evidence on the prevalence of and trends in "lifetime" or long-term employment in the United States for cohorts ending their careers between 1969 and 2004. I depart from earlier work on long-term employment in the United States by focusing on measures of tenure in the longest job ever held for several cohorts of workers near the end of their working lives. This provides a natural and direct measure of the frequency of long-term employment. In contrast to more commonly used measures of workers' tenure on their current job or annual turnover, this retrospective measure of the length of workers' longest jobs speaks directly to the prevalence of long-term employment relationships over the course of workers' entire careers.

By using both these retrospective measures and different data sets than previous studies of job stability, this study covers a longer time span, adding slightly more historical perspective on the significance of recent changes. Most previous studies have relied on Current Population Study (CPS) files or longitudinal data, such as the Panel Study of Income Dynamics, from which consistent tenure data are available only from the mid-1970s forward. Many of these studies are also complicated by changes in question wording of several of the key tenure measures, which may make comparability over time difficult.

I use data from three different data sets to estimate the distribution of tenure on the longest job ever held, from cohorts of workers observed within two years of age sixty between 1969 and 2004. Specifically, data are drawn from the Retirement History Survey (RHS), started in 1969; the National Longitudinal Study of Older Men (NLS), started in 1966; and the Health and Retirement Study (HRS), started in 1992. From each of these surveys, I construct a measure of tenure on the longest job a worker has ever held, from questions that (with one exception discussed below) are quite consistent over time. I examine cohorts of men who are aged fifty-eight to sixty-two years in each of the years 1969, 1975, 1980, 1992, 1998, and 2004. Because the first two data sets are available only for men (or only partially available for women), I limit my analysis to men, for whom there is the strongest suspicion of declining employment stability.

Several findings emerge from this study. First, the length of workers' longest jobs has changed very little for male workers completing their careers between 1969 and 2004. Average tenure on the longest job is approximately twenty-two years in both 1969 and 2004. Second, the endpoints over which these trends are calculated are quite important to this conclusion. If, in particular, trends are considered for a later period starting in 1975 or 1980, there is evidence of a decline of two to four years in longest tenure. Third, using regression analysis to forecast future cohorts' longest tenure as they approach age sixty provides additional evidence of some decline in long-term employment. Finally, while there is some evidence of recent changes in the probability of having a long-term job, it remains the case that most male workers in the United States can expect to remain with one employer for at least twenty years, suggesting that conventional wisdom may overstate the case for structural changes in U.S. employment relationships.

CURRENT FINDINGS ON TRENDS IN JOB TENURE

The question of whether job stability has declined in the United States, and the tendency for academic studies and the popular press to disagree over its answer, have been around since at least the mid-1990s. A collection of empirical research related to this controversy is contained in a collection of studies from 2000 edited by David Neumark.[4]

Neumark summarized several empirical investigations of changes in job stability and/or job security covering the period from the mid-1970s through the mid-1990s. Most of the studies included in his volume point to some modest increase in turnover (or some decline in average tenure), for some worker groups, during some subset of the years between 1970 and 1995. However, what is clearly *not* found is consistent evidence of a major change in the dynamics of worker–firm relationships. Neumark (p. 23) thus concludes that it would be "premature to infer long-term trends towards declines in long-term employment relationships."

Some more recent studies have found evidence of declining current job tenure during the 1990s, based on the CPS and other data sources. For example, Leora Friedberg and Michael Owyang show that current job tenure for men declined by approximately one year between 1983 and 1998, using data from the Survey of Consumer Finances.[5] It is not clear, however, that a decline of one year in current tenure suggests a major change in the underlying employment relationship. They also show much larger changes in measures of expected job tenure among current workers. A more recent and extensive study by Henry Farber, using more years of data from the CPS, documents a decline in current tenure among men, starting with cohorts born in the 1940s.[6] Farber also compares current tenure among employed men born from the 1920s through the 1970s and shows that, adjusting for age and a variety of other factors, cohorts starting with those born in the 1950s have current job tenure that is 35% to 40% lower than that of cohorts born in the 1920s.

My study differs from prior work mainly in the measure of employment stability that is used. I focus on groups of men who are observed near the end of their working lives, and utilize retrospective data on their completed (or nearly completed) tenure in the longest job ever held. As noted above, there are several advantages of this approach. First, it avoids the need to translate from job retention rates or distributions of current tenure into measures that speak directly to the frequency of long-term employment relationships. If, for example, similar fractions of workers at the end of their working lives in 1969 and in 2004 have been with a single employer for more than twenty years, it is difficult to argue that the prevalence of long-term employment relationships has changed.

A second advantage is that, while the data I use nominally span only a slightly longer period of time than previous work (1969 to 2004), they make comparisons that effectively include many earlier years. Measures of tenure in the longest job for the initial cohort observed in 1969, for example, will summarize the turnover probabilities faced by workers from the 1930s through the 1960s. One concern with many of the previous studies is that consistently collected data from prior to the mid-1970s are virtually nonexistent.

The primary disadvantage of the approach used here is that measure of tenure on the longest job will, of course, directly reflect workers' entire careers only for those individuals who are close to the end of their careers. Tenure on the longest job ever held by a thirty-five-year-old, for example, will not reflect the likelihood that a current job may *eventually* last for many years. For this reason, I utilize data focused on older workers, and look only at workers who are between fifty-eight and sixty-two years of age. The drawback of this is that fairly recent changes in employment relationships may not yet be evident in my sample of older workers, particularly if recent cohorts of older workers were at least partially insulated from these changes. I consider this possibility in the final section, and show that there is evidence of declining employment stability if I include a broader set of workers whose careers are still in progress in 2004.

DATA

Before presenting my basic empirical findings, I briefly describe the three data sets used.

The Retirement History Survey (RHS) began in 1969 with a survey of approximately eleven thousand men and unmarried women aged fifty-eight to sixty-three. While these individuals were reinterviewed every other year until 1980, I rely primarily on information collected at the first survey wave. To maintain consistency with later cohorts drawn from other data sets, I look at the subsample of men aged fifty-eight to sixty-two in the initial year, 1969.

The main questions of interest for this chapter come from a section of the survey that collects retrospective information on previous jobs held. In particular, survey respondents are asked a series of questions about the longest job they ever held, including the year in which that job started and the year in which it ended. From these questions, I calculate tenure in the longest job held.

NATIONAL LONGITUDINAL SURVEY OF OLDER MEN

The National Longitudinal Survey of Older Men (NLS) began in 1966 by surveying a sample of men aged forty-five to fifty-nine in that year. Because of the much broader age range in the NLS survey than in the RHS, I use the NLS to construct three separate cohorts of older men, observed in three different calendar years. Specifically, I look at the distribution of tenure on the longest job for: (1) men aged fifty-eight to sixty-two in 1969 (for comparison with the RHS results), (2) men aged fifty-eight to sixty-two in 1975, and (3) men aged fifty-eight to sixty-two in 1980.

The key questions used from this data set are similar to those from the RHS. In particular, individuals in the initial year of the NLS were asked for the dates at which their longest previous job started and ended, as well as the date at which their current job started. In each subsequent year of the NLS survey, individuals are asked whether they are still with the same employer as in the previous survey wave. If they are not, they are asked about when their current job started, and about any intervening jobs completed between the current and previous survey. To code tenure in the longest job for each of the three cohorts in 1969, 1975, and 1980, I utilize data on both the longest job held at the initial survey year and updates from the longitudinal data.

Finally, the Health and Retirement Study (HRS) began in 1992 with a survey of individuals ages fifty to sixty-one and their spouses. These individuals have been resurveyed every other year since then. In addition to the initial HRS cohorts born between 1931 and 1941, later years of the survey have included those born from 1942 through 1953. This allows me to define three cohorts from the HRS: (1) men aged fifty-eight to sixty-two in 1992, (2) men aged fifty-eight to sixty-two in 1998, and (3) men aged fifty-eight to sixty-two in 2004.

There is one substantive difference from the earlier data sets in the survey question used in the HRS to capture tenure in the longest job. In the first wave of the HRS, individuals are asked about their current job (if currently employed) or their previous job (if not currently employed). Then, individuals are asked whether they had some previous job that lasted for at least five years, along with how many such jobs they have held. If there are multiple previous jobs lasting for five years or more, the individual is asked for starting and ending dates only for the *most recent* of these jobs. Because the other surveys ask specifically about the length of the longest job ever held, there is the potential for the calculated length of longest job in the HRS to be understated. If, for example, an individual worked at one previous job for ten years, and then at a subsequent job for six years prior to the initial HRS wave, we would miss the longest job tenure because of the structure of the questions. Analysis across data sets shows that, for most workers, the most recent long-term job is also the longest job, and so this question difference in the HRS is unlikely to result in significant bias. I investigate this in more detail and, as explained below, find that this seems unlikely to affect my estimated trends.

RESULTS: THE DISTRIBUTION OF TENURE
ON THE LONGEST JOB, 1969–2004

The basic facts about long-term employment among U.S. men are summarized in table 2.1. Each column presents summary measures of the distribution of longest tenure among men aged fifty-eight to sixty-two for a different survey year. Because these tabulations are based on a fixed age group, the columns can also be thought of as reflecting different five-year birth cohorts of men. For convenience, the table also lists the midpoint of the birth years of the men on which each column is based. Among men born in the five years centered around 1909, average and median tenure on the longest job are approximately twenty-two years. Similarly, for the cohort born around 1944, average and median longest tenure remain at twenty-two years.

A potentially important point, given the large number of studies of employment stability that begin with data from the 1970s or early 1980s, is that longest tenure does increase to approximately twenty-four years for those cohorts observed at age fifty-eight to sixty-two in 1975 and 1980. As a result, there appears to be a reduction in average tenure if we compare current rates of long-term employment with those prevailing in the mid-1970s or early 1980s, as many previous studies have done. This downward trend, however, does not remain when earlier birth cohorts (observed in 1969) are included. The picture that emerges from the full set of years covered in table 2.1 is not consistent with a major break in the prevalence of long-term employment among men in the United States over the past thirty years.

The fraction of men with longest tenure below ten, twenty, or thirty years are similarly inconsistent with a reduction in the importance of long-term employment relationships. Much of the recent rhetoric has suggested that a typical worker should no longer expect to remain with one employer for a significant fraction of his or her career. For all of the cohorts represented in table 2.1, however, more than half of the men conclude their careers with twenty or more years with a single employer, and around a quarter have thirty or more years of tenure on their longest job.

To compare these results with earlier estimates of long-term employment probabilities, note that an important study by Robert Hall originally argued that stable, "near-lifetime" employment was quite prevalent in the United States, based on the empirical finding that approximately 37% of men were in jobs that would eventually last for more than twenty years.[7] My estimates emphasize even more strongly the likelihood that most workers will have *some* job during their working lives that lasts for more than twenty years. Most comparable to the results presented here, Hall reports that among male workers aged fifty-five and over, roughly 50% will have eventual job tenure of twenty or more years. The results in table 2.1 show that this remains true for workers completing their careers in the past few years, just as it was for those retiring in the early 1970s.

SURVEY YEAR	1969	1969	1975	1980	1992	1998	2004
AVERAGE BIRTH YEAR	1909	1909	1915	1920	1932	1938	1944
DATA SOURCE	RHS	NLS	NLS	NLS	HRS	HRS	HRS
ALL MEN							
Mean (years)	21.9	22.3	23.8	24.1	22.7	21.8	21.8
Median (years)	21	22	24	24	23	22	22
% <= 10 years	17.9	15.8	12.5	9.5	14.9	16	17.8
% <= 20 years	48.3	47.5	39.8	36.9	41.4	45.2	45.1
% <=30 years	75.6	75.6	72.4	72.7	72.1	76.1	74.5
N =	6884	1204	1341	968	1298	1513	821
NON-WHITES							
Mean (years)	18.3	18.7	22.0	23.0	19.4	20.0	18.8
Median (years)	17	18	21	25	20	20	17
% <= 10 years	27.4	25.9	14.9	12.1	18.8	19.1	23.9
% <= 20 years	59.2	57.1	48.0	37.3	52.1	51.5	58.3
% <=30 years	86.7	85.2	78.4	78.6	86.4	79.9	84.4
N =	625	369	388	261	234	257	140
WHITES							
Mean (years)	22.2	22.6	24.0	24.2	23.1	22.1	22.3
Median (years)	21	22	24	24	24	22	23
% <= 10 years	17.0	14.8	12.3	9.3	14.4	15.6	16.6
% <= 20 years	47.3	46.6	38.8	37.0	39.9	44.4	42.9
% <= 30 years	74.5	74.7	71.7	72.3	70.2	75.6	72.9
N =	6215	835	953	707	1064	1256	678

All entries are based on tabulations using sampling weights, for the cohort of men aged 58 to 62 in the given survey year.

Table 2.1   Tenure on the longest job, 1969–2004

The remaining rows of table 2.1 show the pattern of longest tenure over time when each cohort is split according to race. Because of small sample sizes, the men are divided only into white and nonwhite groups. Among both racial groups, tenure in the longest job is again quite stable when looking at the end points, but rises for the middle cohorts. The rise (1969–1980) and decline (1980–2004) are particularly steep for nonwhites. Median tenure among nonwhite males goes from seventeen years in 1979 to a high of twenty-five years in 1980, and then returns to seventeen years by 2004. The increase in longest tenure for the group observed in 1980 is notable since it suggests that, for this cohort, longest tenure is actually higher among nonwhites than among whites. These findings confirm (with the exception of 1980) that nonwhite males are substantially less likely than white males to remain with a single employer for many years. Nearly 60% of nonwhite males have tenure in the longest job of less than twenty years in 2004, compared to just 45% of white males, and median tenure in the longest job is five years lower among nonwhites (for a median of seventeen years) than among whites. Over time, both groups show little change in tenure on the longest job between 1969 and 2004.

Although not shown in table 2.1, I have also tabulated these tenure measures separately by men's level of education. Because many of the changes in the economy over the past thirty years have had differential impacts on more- and less-skilled workers, it is interesting to see whether there are differential changes in tenure by skill level. Among men with twelve or more years of education the story is very similar to that for the entire sample: longest tenure initially rises and then falls somewhat, so that the starting and ending points both show a median of twenty-two years of tenure. Among men with less than a high school education, there is evidence of a decline in tenure. Average tenure in the longest job goes from approximately 21 years in 1969 to 18.6 years in 2004, with median tenure falling from 21 to 17 years over the same period.

The decline in median tenure among those with less than a high school education must be viewed in light of dramatic increases in educational attainment over this period. This is important because the fraction of each cohort defined as "less educated" is shrinking over time. Having less than a high school degree in 2004 places a worker at a much lower point in the overall distribution of education than it did in 1969. In additional tabulations, I find that the decline in tenure among the less educated goes away if I use a relative measure of education that changes over time as average education improves. If I focus on the bottom 25% of the distribution of years of education, rather than a fixed cutoff of twelve years, there is no evidence of a decline in longest tenure between 1969 and 2004.

LOOKING BEYOND SUMMARY STATISTICS:
DATA CONCERNS AND BROADER LABOR FORCE CHANGES

Despite the finding of relative stability in tenure on the longest job, it is important to ask whether any underlying trends or data issues could be obscuring changes over time. Caution is always required when making comparisons over time based on different data sets in different years.[8] It is not possible to prove conclusively that the datasets are strictly comparable over time, but I next address two specific concerns about comparability in these data. More importantly, trends in the labor market could have offsetting effects on the distribution of tenure, and could affect the interpretation of changes (or lack thereof) in the tenure distributions.

One pattern that stands out in table 2.1 is that tenure in the longest job appears to increase from 1969 to 1975, but then levels off or falls after 1980. This peak is particularly steep among nonwhite men and is entirely driven by data from the later two NLS cohorts. One possible explanation for these increases in longest tenure across the NLS cohorts involves sample attrition from the NLS. It is well-documented that attrition from the NLS cohort of older men was significant, particularly during the 1970s and 1980s.[9] If those who leave the survey (and so are not observed in 1975 and 1980) tend to have lower job tenure than those who remain (which comparisons of tenure in the years prior to attrition suggest is the case), this attrition from the sample could produce an apparent, but spurious, increase in longest tenure over time.

To examine the extent to which sample attrition may account for the peak in longest tenure during 1975 and 1980, I estimate longest tenure in 1969 for individuals who do not respond in the later years of the survey. Specifically, I take tenure on the longest job as of the final year an individual responds to the survey, and use this to replace the missing observation in 1980 (and similarly for those who do not respond in 1975). This will understate their true longest tenure by 1980, since this value can only increase over time, and so will provide a lower bound on the true distribution of longest tenure among the entire cohort present in the sample as of 1969. Following this procedure still produces substantially higher tenure in 1975 and 1980 compared to 1969. This suggests that the increase in longest tenure among cohorts completing their careers in the second half of the 1970s is not an artifact of sample attrition.

A second data issue to consider is the extent to which a difference between the tenure questions in the HRS and the other data sets could lead to an understatement of longest tenure for the men observed in 1992, 1998, and 2004. As noted above, the HRS collects information on tenure in the most recent job lasting more than five years, rather than explicitly asking for the longest of all previous jobs. This could lead to an apparent finding that tenure is low in the 1990s and 2004 relative to previous decades, since the data sets covering those earlier decades ask specifically about the longest job ever held.

To estimate the quantitative importance of this data issue, I use several additional variables from the job history section of the HRS. Specifically, I use information on the number of jobs an individual had that lasted for five or more years, and information on when the most recent of these jobs (and the only one for which actual tenure information was reported) began. Briefly, if a worker's most recent previous job suggests that much of his work history is unaccounted for by the current and previous job recorded in the HRS, it is possible that another (unreported) job is actually his longest. In such cases, I assume that longest tenure is actually the entire span of labor-force participation not yet accounted for, to get an upper bound on the true tenure on the longest job. This exercise increases median tenure on the longest job in the HRS by approximately one year. While the longest tenure distributions in the HRS are thus probably slightly understated, the magnitude of this understatement is modest, certainly less than one year.[10]

Potentially more important than details of data collection are changes over the past several decades in the behavior and labor market experiences of these cohorts. Specifically, differences across the cohorts in age of retirement, educational attainment, and veteran status could produce changes in length of longest tenure when no underlying change in the nature of employment relationships has occurred (or could obscure actual changes).

Table 2.2 summarizes several characteristics of the different cohorts of men. First, there is a strong trend towards earlier retirement. Among men fifty-eight to sixty-two years old observed in 1969, between 4% and 6% had already retired. By 2004, however, more than one-third of the cohort reports themselves as retired. This is consistent with much earlier work documenting a long-term trend in the United States towards earlier retirement.[11]

The trend towards earlier retirement could have a simple mechanical effect on tenure in the longest job, particularly if most of the longest jobs are also the last jobs workers hold before retiring. If the total lifetime length of labor-force participation is reduced by several years from the earliest to the latest cohorts considered here, we might also expect a reduction in tenure in the longest job. In 1992, for example, 61% of the observed

BIRTH YEAR	1909	1909	1915	1920	1932	1938	1944
DATA SOURCE	RHS	NLS	NLS	NLS	HRS	HRS	HRS
Percent retired:	5.6	4.0	18.0	26.9	29.6	35.7	37.1
Average age:	59.9	59.9	60.0	60.4	59.4	59.9	60.0
Average yrs of education:	10.1	9.8	10.4	11.0	12.3	12.7	13.4
Percent veterans:*	25.7	25.7	50.5	77.1	70.3	46.3	4.16

All entries are based on tabulations using sampling weights, for the cohort of men aged 58 to 62 in the given survey year.
* Percent veterans comes from tabulations in Bound and Turner (1999) and is for white males only.

Table 2.2   Characteristics across cohorts observed, 1969–2004

cohort who are still employed report that they are currently working in their longest job. As workers end their careers sooner, even without any corresponding change in the underlying stability of employment relationships, we should also see some decline in the tenure measure used here.

To approximate how much changes in retirement age affect longest job tenure, I create a counterfactual distribution of tenure that holds the fraction already retired constant at approximately 5%. First, I calculate the number of years since retirement for those individuals who are already retired by 1992, 1998, or 2004. Approximately 85% of those already retired in 1992 would still have been working if the age of retirement had not changed between 1969 and 1992. For these men, I add the number of years since retirement to their reported longest tenure. This will overstate the effect of reduced retirement age on my measure of tenure in the longest job, since some of the longest jobs have been completed several years prior to retirement. For all men, this simulation raises average tenure on the longest job in the HRS by approximately one year. Thus, the conclusion of stability in longest tenure between 1969 and 2004 would likely be modified to one of a small increase in longest tenure if reductions in the retirement age had not occurred.

The increase in educational attainment is another striking change in the older male labor force during this time period shown in table 2.2. Average education among the different cohorts of men rises substantially over the period examined here. Average years of education for the fifty-eight- to sixty-two-year-old men observed in 1969 is just 10.1 years; by 2004 the cohort of the same age has average educational attainment of 13.4 years. How might this rising educational attainment affect eventual tenure on the longest job? There could again be a direct, mechanical effect, similar to that arising from changes in the retirement age. As individuals spend more time in school, holding all else constant, total time in the labor market will decline, and so we would expect some reduction in tenure on the longest job, even without any change in employment stability over the life cycle. The trends in educational attainment and retirement ages, taken together, suggest that men born in the 1940s will be in the labor force for two to four fewer years than those born around 1910. As was the case with the trends towards earlier retirement, this suggests that tenure in the longest job might have fallen slightly even without a major change in the employer–employee relationship.

It is also reasonable to expect that higher educational attainment could lead to an increase in longest tenure, since more-educated individuals are more likely to hold long-term jobs. The magnitude of this difference, however, does not seem to be enough to modify the basic results. I have used regression analysis to examine trends in average tenure across the cohorts, controlling for average levels of education. Controlling for changes in education levels has no noticeable effect on the estimated trends.

A final potentially important change across the cohorts of men studied here is in the fraction of men who took time out of the civilian labor force to serve in the military. Because there are relatively large differences across cohorts in the fraction of men who are veterans, this could also affect patterns of longest-job tenure. A period of military service could, for example, delay the job-shopping process, and result in men starting their career jobs later in life. If cohorts with unusually high levels of military service are also those with unusually short tenure, this could confound my attempt to measure changes in the underlying employment relationships.

It is difficult to investigate this issue directly with the current data sets, because the RHS and the NLS do not contain information on military service. Fortunately, data are available from other sources on the fraction of various birth cohorts who have completed some military service. John Bound and Sarah Turner report the fraction of white males in the corresponding birth cohorts who had some military service, taken from 1980 Census data.[12] Their results are repeated in table 2.2 here, and show that the fraction of veterans is particularly high for those men that I observe in 1980 and 1992 (birth cohorts centered around the years 1920 and 1932). Thus, the possibility that earlier cohorts have artificially low tenure due to higher rates of military service is ruled out. On the contrary, it is precisely those cohorts with the highest levels of tenure (and in the middle of the period studied) that also have the highest probabilities of past military service.

RECONCILING WITH OTHER FINDINGS, AND LOOKING TO THE FUTURE

Most of the analysis presented thus far is at odds with the widespread view of substantial erosion in long-term employment relationships in recent years. As noted above, it is possible that very recent changes will not be apparent in my tabulations of longest tenure from workers at the very end of their careers. In this section, I extend my analysis based on the HRS to make fuller use of slightly younger individuals observed in that data set. This is helpful both for forecasting how longest tenure may evolve in the near future, and for reconciling these results with other recent studies.

Before moving to the additional data analysis, two points about my results so far are important to note. First, results in table 2.1 show that conclusions about trends in employment stability may be somewhat sensitive to the starting and ending points of particular studies. Without the observations for men from 1969, in particular, there would appear to be a modest decline in tenure on the longest job between 1975 and 2004. Second, if job-changing rates increased in the mid-to-late 1990s, the most recent cohort considered here (sixty-year-olds in 2004) would already have accumulated substantial job tenure and may have been somewhat insulated from these changes.

To examine whether my focus on completed careers obscures recent changes, I make use of the fuller sample from the HRS. The HRS currently surveys individuals born between 1921 and 1953, and includes a slightly broader range of birth years due to inclusion of spouses of respondents. In this section, I use all of these observations from the HRS and estimate simple regressions similar to those reported in Farber's 2007 study.[13] Specifically, Farber uses regression to hold constant workers' age and other characteristics, and then reports cohort-specific changes in the length of the current job. For all individuals observed in the HRS between 1992 and 2004, covering birth cohorts from 1915 to 1953, I estimate a version of Farber's equation 1:

$$ln(T_{ijk}) = C_j + A_k + \varepsilon_{ijk}$$

The dependent variable is the log of either current tenure or tenure on the longest job. These measures are regressed on dummies for birth cohorts (C_j), current years of age (A_k), and in some cases additional controls for demographics and education. Because I have a much smaller data set, with fewer workers observed in any particular age by birth cohort cell, I use ten-year birth cohort groups. When the log of current tenure is the dependent variable, most directly replicating Farber's analysis, my results are very consistent with his. Specifically, men born in the 1940s and 1950s have current tenure that is from 20% to 35% lower than the cohort born in 1915. I next estimate the same regression with tenure on the longest job as the dependent variable. This regression shows that tenure on the longest job has declined by 10% to 25% between birth cohorts of men from 1915 and those born in the 1940s and 1950s. These regressions also allow me to control for a variety of additional characteristics, including race, education, ethnicity, and veteran status; this does not substantially change the estimated trends in longest tenure.

Why do these regression results based on HRS data show a decline, in contrast to the simple means presented in table 2.1? First, this is partially a function of the birth cohorts covered in the HRS. The earliest cohorts included in these regressions were born in approximately 1915, and so they are most similar to a comparison of means that ignores the first two columns of table 2.1. Second, using the expanded HRS also allows me to include slightly younger workers, who have not yet reached age sixty by 2004. Men born after 1945 show the largest reductions in tenure on the longest job, and these men are not included in the analysis in table 2.1.

A natural question to ask at this point is whether the simple comparison of means or the regression-based estimate is most preferred. The regression analysis allows for using more of the HRS data, since I can statistically adjust for age rather than limiting the analysis to those who are observed around age sixty. On the other hand, it is not possible to directly incorporate the observations from the NLS and RHS into the

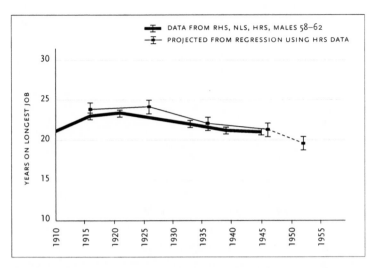

Figure 2.1   Tenure on the longest job: males at age 60, by birth cohort

regression analysis. Finally, the regression analysis relies on assumptions concerning the evolution of longest tenure across cohorts and ages. Specifically, it assumes that the shape of the age profile of longest tenure, or how longest tenure evolves as workers age, does not change across cohorts. More importantly, figure 2.1 shows that these two sets of analysis are largely consistent with one another. The thick black line shows average tenure in the longest job for men, taken from table 2.1, based on observations of birth cohorts when they reach age sixty. The grey line connects predictions of longest tenure for several birth cohorts of men predicted from the regression coefficients estimated with only the HRS data, as described earlier in this section. The figure also shows 95% confidence intervals around both sets of estimates.

Figure 2.1 shows that the HRS regression-based predictions show both slightly higher tenure and a slightly steeper decline between the 1915 cohort and later cohorts. Generally, however, the patterns are similar, and the confidence intervals for the two series overlap. Note that the regression coefficients can be used to predict what longest tenure will be when the men born around 1951 reach age sixty. These predictions are represented by the right-most point in the figure, where the dotted line connecting them indicates that these are out-of-sample projections. That is, this cohort is not observed at age sixty, and so this prediction depends critically on the assumption of no change in the age profile of longest tenure. Focusing on these predictions for the cohort born in 1951 suggests that longest tenure will fall to around twenty years for individuals reaching age sixty in 2011. This does suggest that some of the change in employment stability is not yet evident if we limit our focus to relatively old workers.

To conclude, I return to the question raised and assertions made by media discussions of employment stability. Has lifetime employment largely disappeared as a feature of the U.S. labor market? The clear answer to this question is no. Even the most pessimistic evidence presented above suggests that male workers retiring in the next few years will end their careers with an average of two decades with a single employer. Has there, however, been a decline in the prevalence of lifetime employment? The answer to this question appears to be yes, with the decline occurring quite recently. Men who will retire in the next several years will have tenure on their longest job that is roughly 25% lower than cohorts who retired in the mid-1970s. This decline is probably tempered to something closer to a 10% reduction if the comparison is instead made to men who retired in the late 1960s.

Concurrent changes in the labor market should be kept in mind in interpreting these trends. In particular, men who complete their careers in 2008 and later have been in the labor force for substantially fewer years than their earlier counterparts, as the result of spending more years in school and retiring earlier. Thus, it should not come as a surprise that their time with a career employer is somewhat shorter as well. Taken together, the magnitude of observed declines in long-term employment and the reduction in total years in the labor force suggest caution in concluding that employment relationships in the United States have undergone a major structural change.

NOTES

1   Julie Connelly, "Youthful Attitudes, Sobering Realities," *New York Times*, October 29, 2003.

2   William J. Holstein, "Office Space: Armchair MBA; Job Insecurity, From the Chief Down," *New York Times*, March 27, 2005.

3   Schmidt, Stefanie R., "Job Security Beliefs in the General Social Survey: Evidence on Long-Run Trends and Comparability with Other Surveys" in *On the Job: Is Long-Term Employment a Thing of the Past?*, ed. David Neumark (New York: Russell Sage Foundation, 2000).

4   David Neumark, ed., *On the Job: Is Long-Term Employment a Thing of the Past?* (New York: Russell Sage Foundation, 2000).

5   Leora Freidberg and Michael T. Owyang, "Explaining the Evolution of Pension Structure and Job Tenure," Working Paper (Federal Reserve Bank of St. Louis, 2004).

6   Henry Farber, "Is the Company Man an Anachronism?" in *The Price of Independence: The Economics of Early Adulthood*, ed. Sheldon Danziger and Cecelia Rouse (New York: Russell Sage Foundation, 2007). See also his chapter in this volume.

7   Robert Hall, "The Importance of Lifetime Jobs in the U.S. Economy," *American Economic Review* 72 (1982): 716–24.

8   Even when using the same data set, such as the CPS, there is a possibility that changes in question wording or other survey methodology could lead to spurious time series comparisons.

9   See, for example, U.S. Department of Labor, Bureau of Labor Statistics, *NLS Handbook* 2003.

10 This is an upper bound on the potential error in the HRS measures since the years not covered by a recent or current long-term job may also be split among several relatively short jobs. This is especially likely since the unaccounted-for jobs occur early in workers' careers, when job changing is more frequent.

11 See, for example, Richard Burkhauser and Joseph Quinn, "Has the Early Retirement Trend Reversed?" (unpublished manuscript, Boston College, 1997).

12 John Bound and Sarah Turner, "Going to War and Going to College: Did World War II and the G.I. Bill Increase Education Attainment for Returning Veterans?" *Journal of Labor Economics* 20 (2002): 784–815.

13 Farber, "Is the Company Man an Anachronism?"

CHAPTER THREE

Hurt the Worst | *The Risk of Unemployment among Disadvantaged and Advantaged Male Workers, 1968–2003*

BENJAMIN J. KEYS & SHELDON DANZIGER

Over the last three decades, structural changes in the American labor market eliminated many highly paid, stable jobs that had previously been available to workers with a high school diploma or less. Even though unemployment rates for much of the past decade have been lower than they were from the mid-1970s through the early 1990s, the relative economic position of less-educated male workers is lower now than it was a quarter century ago. For example, among workers between the ages of fifteen and fifty-four who where high school dropouts, real hourly wage rates in 2004 were 9% below their 1979 levels; among high school graduates in the same age range, real wages in 2004 were only 5% higher than in 1979.[1] Declines in the extent of unionization, erosion of the real value of the minimum wage, increased globalization of labor and product markets, increased immigration, and a technology-driven wage premium for college graduates have all contributed to the labor market problems of less-educated workers.[2]

Job security is important, particularly for disadvantaged workers who have fewer financial resources to cushion income losses than other workers and are less able to plan for the future when jobs are insecure. Job losses have more deleterious consequences for less-educated workers who are less likely than other workers to receive severance packages and more likely than others to have difficulty finding new jobs. This chapter addresses several questions about changes in employment stability over the last three decades: How likely is it that a man who is employed when interviewed in one year is unemployed when interviewed two years later? Conversely, how likely is it that a man who is unemployed when interviewed in one year is employed when interviewed two years later? Have these probabilities changed over time? Do trends in employment security differ for workers classified by education and race?

We analyze longitudinal data from the Panel Study of Income Dynamics (PSID) for the period from 1968 through 2003. We compare the risk of unemployment for employed male household heads classified by age (20–30, 31–40, 41–50, 51–62), educational attainment (high school dropout, high school diploma, some college, college graduate), and race (white, black). We focus on transitions into and out of unemployment as unemployment most frequently reflects involuntary job loss. We do not analyze individuals who have exited from employment to being out of the labor force because our data do not distinguish between those who left jobs and the labor force for personal reasons, such as to attend school or to retire early, and those who stopped looking for work because they thought no jobs were available (discouraged workers). We find that younger, less educated, and minority male workers have a higher risk of unemployment at the end of a two-year period, and also have a lower probability of returning to work after having been unemployed.

The next section briefly reviews previous studies; later sections describe data and methods, present results, and summarize key findings.

PREVIOUS STUDIES

Because Henry S. Farber reviews the previous literature (see chapter 1, this volume), we mention only studies that are closely related to our analysis.[3] Young workers usually work at a series of jobs after completing their education. Robert H. Topel and Michael P. Ward estimate that a typical male holds seven jobs in his first ten years in the labor market.[4] Thus, we control for a worker's age. Robert W. Fairlie and Lori G. Kletzer document that black men were about 25% more likely to experience job displacement than whites during the 1980s (4.8% vs. 3.8% per year).[5] In addition, black displaced workers were 30% less likely to be reemployed by the next survey (44% vs. 61%). These differences can be attributed partly to the fact that black men had on average completed fewer years of schooling than white men. Thus, we control for racial and educational differences in estimating the risk of unemployment and the likelihood that an unemployed worker returns to employment, and we also calculate the risk of unemployment for separate race and education categories.

Business cycle fluctuations strongly affect the likelihood of job loss. After accounting for business cycle fluctuations, Francis X. Diebold, David Neumark, and Daniel Polsky conclude that job stability was roughly constant over the 1973 to 1991 period.[6] However, job retention rates fell for less educated and African American workers, relative to more educated and white employees. We account for the business cycle by evaluating how the risk of unemployment for various workers is affected by fluctuations in the national unemployment rate and how this risk has varied during each of the last several decades to see if there have been secular trends that are unrelated to cyclical fluctuations.

Our methodology draws heavily from that of two prior studies. Peter Gottschalk and Robert Moffitt analyze three measures of job insecurity: the probability that a job ends involuntarily, the probability of starting a spell of nonemployment (either becoming unemployed or leaving the labor force) conditional on involuntary job loss, and the probability that the subsequent job has lower wages than the involuntarily terminated job.[7] They find that all three probabilities were generally unchanged from the early 1980s through the mid-1990s. Robert G. Valletta finds that between 1976 and 1991, the annual likelihood of involuntary dismissals increased from 4.1% to 5.5% for men, with the unemployment rate being the strongest predictor of dismissals, and that higher job tenure and higher wages are negatively related to the probability of job loss.[8]

Building on these studies, we estimate the effects of business cycles, differences across decades, and demographic characteristics on the likelihood that a man working at one interview is unemployed when interviewed two years later and that an unemployed worker in one year has returned to work two years later. Our study period is longer than those of other authors. We estimate both unemployment and reemployment probabilities, and examine how these probabilities and the factors that influence them vary by race, age, and educational attainment.

DATA AND METHODS

The PSID has followed the same individuals from 1968 to the present. In each year, our sample includes male household heads between the ages of twenty and sixty-two who are not students and who have valid race, gender, and education information. The PSID gathers the employment information we use only from household heads, which means that a young adult living with his parents is not a PSID head and is not included. We analyze the risk of unemployment over the period from 1968 to 2003, using all thirty-five years of the panel data, and extending the results of recent studies through the economic boom of the 1990s and the period of slow economic growth following the 2001 recession.[9]

We define unemployment risk as the likelihood that an individual who is employed at one PSID interview is unemployed at the interview two years later. For any year t, our sample consists of men who worked at the time t-2 interview. We define a man as having exited from employment to unemployment if he was not working but was searching for a job at the time t interview. We define a man as having exited from unemployment to employment if he was unemployed at the time t-2 interview but was working when interviewed at time t.[10]

We now describe trends in employment and unemployment for workers classified by education and race. Then we estimate regressions that control for demographic attributes, the business cycle, and secular trends.[11]

RESULTS

TRENDS

Figure 3.1 shows the employment rate from 1968 through 2003 for male household heads between the ages of twenty and sixty-two, classified by educational attainment. The rate for college graduates (top line) is about 95% for most years between 1968 and the early 1990s; the rate then declined to about 90% after 1994. The employment rates for high school graduates and those with some college (the second and third lines) follow roughly the same pattern, although the long-run decline is somewhat greater. About 95% of high school graduates worked in the late 1960s; the rate fell to about 90% by 1980 and then to around 85% in the early 2000s.

High school dropouts (bottom line) are much less likely than other men to be employed in any year and have experienced the greatest decline over the thirty-five-year period.[12] In the late 1960s, their employment rate was about 90%. It fell to 74% in 1983 due to the severe recession. For the next two decades, their employment rate never exceeded 78%. The gap between the employment rate of college graduates and high school dropouts was four percentage points in 1968, but fifteen points in 2003.[13]

High school dropouts are more likely to be unemployed than those with higher education in any year, and this differential has also grown over time. Figure 3.2 documents that unemployment for dropouts rose from 3.9% in 1968 to 13.8% in 1983. The rate remained above 10% until the economic boom of the 1990s when it fell to 5% in 1997. However by 2003, it had increased back to 10%.

The unemployment rates for high school graduates and heads with some college follow the business cycle. Among high school graduates, unemployment rose from around 2% in the late 1960s to 6.7% during the recession in the early 1970s, and then fell to about 4%, before rising to 10.5% in 1983. The rate fell to less than 5% in the late 1980s, rose to about 8% in 1992 and fell to 3.5% in 1999. The rate for college graduates is roughly flat, around 2% in any interview year. Thus, the less educated are much more likely to lose their jobs due to business cycle fluctuations than are college graduates.

Figure 3.3 shows the employment rate separately for African American and white men. The sharp decline in employment over the thirty-five-year period for blacks is similar to that for all high school dropouts. In the late 1960s, black and white males were employed at similar rates (88% and 92% in 1969, respectively). The racial gap widened to nine percentage points by 1979 (84% vs. 93%) and to thirteen points by 1983 (76% vs. 87%) before narrowing during the 1990s boom. In 2003, only 77% of black male household heads and 86% of whites were employed. As shown below, educational attainment differences contribute to this racial employment gap.

The unemployment rate for African American men exceeds that for whites (figure 3.4). While both series show cyclical patterns, black men are more likely to lose their jobs during economic downturns. The unemployment rate spiked for blacks in the mid-1970s, early 1980s, and early 1990s. Between 1979 and 1983, unemployment rose from 7.7% to 15.4% for blacks and from 1.7% to 6.2% for whites. Between 1997 and 2003, the white rate

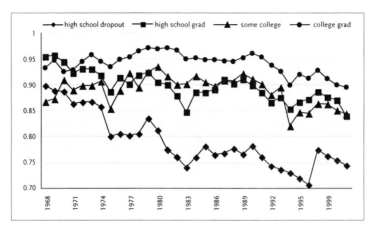

Figure 3.1   Employment rate of male household heads, by education

[Source: Authors' calculations using the PSID, 1968–2003]

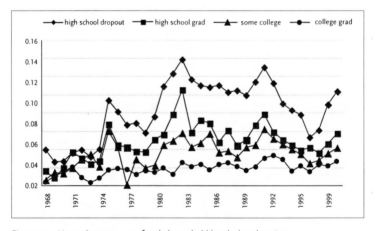

Figure 3.2   Unemployment rate of male household heads, by education

[Source: Authors' calculations using the PSID, 1968–2003]

increased from 2.1% to 3.7%, whereas the black rate increased from 5.7% to 9.4%. These data include only household heads who have lower unemployment rates than other men; also, men between the ages of twenty and sixty-two have lower rates than those of younger and older men.

Figure 3.5 takes advantage of the panel nature of the PSID data and shows the probability that a male employed at the year *t*-2 interview was unemployed at the year *t* interview. This risk of unemployment was highest in 1983—6.9% of men working at the 1981 interview were out of

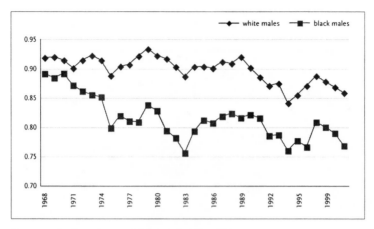

Figure 3.3 Employment rate of male household heads, by race

[Source: Authors' calculations using the PSID, 1968–2003]

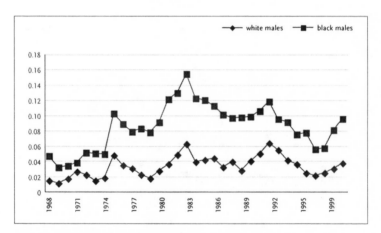

Figure 3.4 Unemployment rate of male household heads, by race

[Source: Authors' calculations using the PSID, 1968–2003]

work and searching for jobs when interviewed two years later. This two-year exit probability fell to 3.6% in 1989, rose to 5.5% in 1992, declined to 2.2% in 1999, and then increased to 4.2% in 2003. The pattern from the early 1980s to the mid-1990s is consistent with changes in the national unemployment rate over the business cycle.

Figure 3.6 shows the probability that an unemployed worker at the *t*-2 interview was working at the year *t* interview. The exit from unemployment to employment is highest in good economic times — the

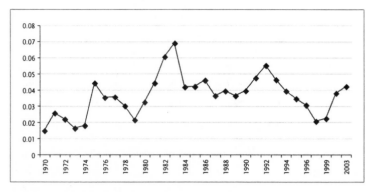

Figure 3.5   Risk of unemployment, male household heads   [Source: Authors' calculations of the probability that a man employed in year t-2 is unemployed when surveyed in year t, using the PSID, 1968–2003]

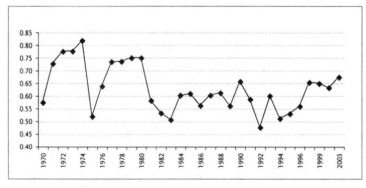

Figure 3.6   Likelihood of returning to work, male household heads   [Source: Authors' calculations of the probability that a man unemployed in year t-2 is employed when surveyed in year t, using the PSID, 1968–2003]

early 1970s, late 1970s, and late 1990s. For instance, among men unemployed in 1981, 50% were employed in 1983; in contrast, among men unemployed in 1997, 65% had returned to work in 1999. The upward trend in recent years, despite the increased risk of unemployment shown in figure 3.5, indicates that the effects of the 2001 recession on the likelihood of reemployment were relatively modest. Unemployed workers have a harder time finding jobs now than in the late 1970s, but have an easier time than in the 1980s and early 1990s.

Regression analysis allows us to identify how age, race, educational attainment, and the business cycle affect the risk of unemployment and the probability that the unemployed return to work that are shown in figures 3.5 and 3.6. The regression coefficients shown in the tables below represent deviations from a baseline exit probability. The baseline worker is defined as a white male college graduate between the ages of fifty-one and sixty-two in the early 2000s. A coefficient greater than one indicates that a man with different attributes (e.g., race or age or education) is more likely to experience an exit than a man with the baseline attributes; a coefficient of less than one indicates that the man is less likely to exit.[14]

REGRESSION RESULTS

Column 1 of table 3.1 shows the regression results for all male household heads between the ages of twenty and sixty-two. The coefficient for high school dropouts, for example, indicates that the risk of unemployment for dropouts was 3.3 times higher than that of college graduates during any two-year period between 1968 and 2003.[15] High school graduates were 1.9 times more likely and those with some college 1.7 times more likely to exit from work to unemployment than college graduates. The risk of unemployment was twice as high for African Americans as whites. Workers between the ages of twenty and thirty were 3.2 times as likely as workers between the ages of fifty-one and sixty-two (the baseline age group) to exit from employment to unemployment. Workers between the ages of thirty-one and forty were twice as likely to exit and those between forty-one and fifty were 1.5 times as likely as older workers.

Like previous studies, we estimate how the risk of unemployment varies over the business cycle, as measured by the year t national unemployment rate. A one percentage point increase in this rate increases a worker's risk of exiting to unemployment by 20.8%. To determine how the risk of unemployment differs by decade, holding the unemployment rate constant, we include indicator variables for the 1970s, 1980s, and 1990s. These indicators identify labor market changes that were independent of business cycle fluctuations. We find an upward secular trend in the risk of unemployment—the coefficients for the 1970s, 1980s, and 1990s indicators are all statistically significant and below one. This means that workers fared better in all three decades than they have during 2001–2003 (the reference years). In the 1970s, the risk of unemployment was only about one-third of the risk in the early 2000s; in the 1990s, the risk was about two-thirds the magnitude of the early 2000s.

We estimate regressions for the risk of unemployment separately for each of four educational attainment groups and present the results in columns 2 through 5 of table 3.1. The coefficients in columns 3 and 4 of

	ALL	HIGH SCHOOL DROPOUT	HIGH SCHOOL GRADUATE	SOME COLLEGE	COLLEGE GRADUATE
BLACK	2.023**	1.694**	2.560**	2.234**	1.575+
	(11.82)	(5.53)	(9.71)	(6.09)	(1.69)
AGE 20–30	3.224**	4.325**	3.074**	2.148**	1.064
	(13.08)	(11.79)	(6.42)	(3.35)	(0.21)
AGE 31–40	2.072**	2.213**	1.922**	2.383**	1.154
	(8.08)	(6.19)	(3.59)	(3.98)	(0.57)
AGE 41–50	1.526**	1.472**	1.476*	1.668*	1.218
	(4.64)	(3.03)	(2.03)	(2.36)	(0.78)
HS DROPOUT	3.321**				
	(11.08)				
HS GRADUATE	1.919**				
	(6.22)				
SOME COLLEGE	1.694**				
	(4.71)				
UNEMPLOYMENT RATE	1.208**	1.200**	1.246**	1.236**	1.040
	(10.81)	(6.67)	(7.21)	(4.65)	(0.67)
1970s	0.367**	0.413**	0.414**	0.460**	0.376**
	(9.31)	(4.08)	(4.91)	(3.41)	(3.04)
1980s	0.549**	0.713	0.549**	0.480**	0.450**
	(5.66)	(1.56)	(3.29)	(3.45)	(2.60)
1990s	0.682**	0.769	0.626**	0.698+	0.801
	(3.84)	(1.25)	(2.80)	(1.81)	(0.91)
OBSERVATIONS	66539	18277	22135	12598	13529

Source: Authors' calculations using the PSID, 1970–2003. Robust z statistics from standard errors clustered at the individual level in parentheses. Sample is of male household heads, age 20–62, who were employed at interview two years earlier. In column 1, the baseline (omitted) category is a white male college graduate aged 51–62 in 2001–2003. In subsequent columns the baseline is a white male aged 51–62 in 2001–2003. The risk of unemployment is calculated as the probability that a man who was employed in year t-2 is unemployed in year t.   + significant at 10%   * significant at 5%   ** significant at 1%

Table 3.1   Risk of unemployment, male household heads (logistic regression analysis)

the top row show that the African American males who are high school graduates and have some college have a greater risk relative to that of their white counterparts. Compared to white high school graduates, African American high school graduates are about 2.5 times more likely to exit to unemployment. African American college graduates are 1.6 times as likely as white college graduates to exit.

Figure 3.1 demonstrated that less-educated workers are at higher risk of unemployment due to cyclical shocks than are more-educated workers. This result is supported in the regression analysis. A one percentage point increase in the unemployment rate increases exits to unemployment among dropouts by 20% and by about 24% for both

	ALL	HIGH SCHOOL DROPOUT	HIGH SCHOOL GRADUATE	SOME COLLEGE	COLLEGE GRADUATE
BLACK	0.483**	0.445**	0.542**	0.376**	1.047
	(7.70)	(5.73)	(3.94)	(3.98)	(0.09)
AGE 20–30	1.510**	1.353	1.700*	1.319	3.539+
	(2.91)	(1.64)	(2.04)	(0.66)	(1.74)
AGE 31–40	1.161	1.055	1.128	1.306	2.199
	(1.02)	(0.27)	(0.45)	(0.67)	(1.25)
AGE 41–50	1.081	1.404	0.892	1.104	0.694
	(0.46)	(1.49)	(0.40)	(0.23)	(0.55)
HS DROPOUT	0.436**				
	(3.26)				
HS GRADUATE	0.576*				
	(2.16)				
SOME COLLEGE	0.752				
	(1.05)				
UNEMPLOYMENT RATE	0.906**	0.864**	0.968	0.860+	1.046
	(3.06)	(3.10)	(0.57)	(1.76)	(0.31)
1970s	1.720**	1.828+	1.441	2.492	1.122
	(2.60)	(1.68)	(1.04)	(1.64)	(0.16)
1980s	1.056	1.411	0.715	1.124	0.920
	(0.26)	(0.97)	(1.00)	(0.25)	(0.12)
1990s	0.840	0.864	0.706	1.209	1.109
	(0.91)	(0.42)	(1.09)	(0.41)	(0.20)
OBSERVATIONS	3714	1658	1222	558	276

Source: Authors' calculations using the PSID, 1970–2003. Robust z statistics from standard errors clustered at the individual level in parentheses. Sample is of male household heads, age 20–62, who were unemployed at interview two years earlier. In column 1, the baseline (omitted) category is a white male college graduate aged 51–62 in 2001–2003. In subsequent columns the baseline is a white male aged 51–62 in 2001–2003. The likelihood of returning to work is calculated as the probability that a man who was unemployed in year t-2 is employed in year t. + significant at 10% * significant at 5% ** significant at 1%

Table 3.2 Likelihood of returning to work, male household heads (logistic regression analysis)

high school graduates and those with some college (columns 2, 3, 4, respectively, table 3.1). In contrast, there is no statistically significant relationship between the unemployment rate and the risk of unemployment for college graduates, who are relatively insulated from business cycle fluctuations (column 5, table 3.1).

Table 3.2 presents regression results parallel to those of table 3.1, except that the dependent variable is the probability that an unemployed worker at the year t-2 interview had returned to work at the year t interview. The first row in column 1 shows that unemployed black men are only about half as likely to return to work as whites. This race effect is large and significant for all education groups except college graduates (coefficients are below 1.0 and significant in columns 2 through 4, but about 1.0 and not significant in column 5). Thus, holding education constant, black workers have a higher risk of unemployment than white workers (table 3.1), and, except for college graduates, are also less likely to find a new job after having lost one (table 3.2).

Workers between the ages of twenty and thirty are 3.2 times more likely to lose a job than fifty-one- to sixty-two-year-olds (table 3.1, column 1), but are 1.5 times more likely to return to work after experiencing unemployment (table 3.2, column 1). Older unemployed workers may pursue new jobs less aggressively, whether because they have access to early retirement benefits or disability benefits or because they are more disillusioned about their employment prospects.

A one percentage point increase in the national unemployment rate is associated with a 10% decline in the likelihood that an unemployed man returns to work (0.906, column 1). This business cycle effect is concentrated among high school dropouts and those who have completed some college (significant coefficients in columns 2 and 4). The probability that unemployed college graduates return to work does not vary significantly with the unemployment rate.

Unemployed workers in the 1970s were about 70% more likely to return to work two years later than were unemployed workers in 2001–2003. Returns to work in the 1980s and 1990s were not significantly different than in the most recent years.

VARIATIONS IN PREDICTED EXIT PROBABILITIES

We use the regression coefficients from a specification like the one shown in table 3.1, but with separate regressions for whites and blacks, to estimate predicted probabilities of the risk of unemployment for a baseline worker between the ages of twenty and thirty, for a hypothetical year during the 1990s, assuming that the unemployment rate was 6%, the mean for the 1968–2003 period. These results are shown in table 3.3. The baseline probability for a worker in each educational attainment category is shown in the top row of the top panel for white men and the top row of the bottom panel for black men.

The risk of unemployment between two years falls as education increases. White high school dropouts have a risk of unemployment of 8.8%, compared to 1.8% for college graduates. For blacks, the risk of unemployment falls from 19.3% for high school dropouts to 6.3% for

	HIGH SCHOOL DROPOUT	HIGH SCHOOL GRADUATE	SOME COLLEGE	COLLEGE GRADUATE
WHITE MALE BASELINE				
Baseline	8.8	3.9	3.3	1.8
Age 31–40	5.2	2.6	3.8	1.8
1970s	5.4	2.5	1.9	1.0
1980s	7.5	3.3	2.5	1.3
2001–2003	12.9	4.1	4.0	2.3
Min. unemployment (3.5)	4.4	1.9	2.3	1.6
Max. unemployment (9.7)	18.9	8.9	5.1	2.0
BLACK MALE BASELINE				
Baseline	19.3	10.4	6.3	*
Age 31–40	9.9	6.4	6.8	*
1970s	10.3	7.3	5.9	*
1980s	18.7	9.5	3.9	*
2001–2003	21.0	22.5	11.0	*
Min. unemployment (3.5)	14.7	6.5	2.5	*
Max. unemployment (9.7)	26.1	17.7	17.5	*

Source: Authors' calculations using PSID, 1970–2003. These use the specification from columns 2–5 of table 3.1 (estimated separately for whites and blacks) to predict exits to unemployment. Sample is restricted to male household heads, age 20–62, who were employed in the interview two years prior. Baseline individual is a male head of household between the ages of 20–30, in the 1990s with the mean unemployment rate over the 1968–2003 period. There are too few black college graduates in the PSID (about 38 per year) to make a meaningful prediction.

Table 3.3   Predicted risk of unemployment, male household heads

those with some college. There are too few black college graduates in the PSID sample to reliably estimate their risk of unemployment.

The racial gap in the risk of unemployment is large—holding education constant, a black worker is about twice as likely to exit to unemployment as a white man. For high school graduates, the risk of unemployment is 10.4% for a young black man and 3.9% for a young white man.

A comparison of the first two rows in each panel of table 3.3 shows that workers ages twenty to thirty have a higher risk of unemployment than those ages thirty-one to forty, for those with a high school degree or less. Among those with some college or a college degree, the age effect is negligible.

Rows 3 through 5 in each panel show how the risk of unemployment varies over recent decades. The risk is highest in the 2001–2003 period and lower in the 1970s and 1980s. For example, the unemployment risk for a young white high school graduate increased from 2.5% in the 1970s to 3.3% in the 1980s to 3.9% in the 1990s to 4.1% in the recent period. For a young black high school graduate, the unemployment risk over these periods rose from 7.3% to 9.5% to 10.4% to 22.5%.

The bottom two rows in each panel of table 3.3 document that there are large business cycle effects for less-educated workers. An increase in the national unemployment rate from 3.5% to 9.7%—the best and worst rates over the thirty-five-year study period—raises the risk of unemployment from 1.9% to 8.9% for white high school graduates and from 6.5% to 17.7% for black high school graduates.

In table 3.4, we use regression coefficients like those in table 3.2, but estimated separately for white and black men, to compute predicted probabilities of exiting from unemployment back into employment. The baseline worker is again a male household head between the ages of twenty and thirty in the 1990s, evaluated at the mean unemployment rate over the study period. Larger numbers represent better outcomes, indicating the likelihood that a worker who was unemployed at the interview two years ago was working at the current interview.

The most educated are much more likely to return to work than the least educated. For example, 88.8% of unemployed white college graduates return to work compared to 68.5% of high school dropouts. About two-thirds of unemployed blacks with some college, but only 39.6% of black high school dropouts returned to work.

The racial gap in returning to work is large among those with a high school degree or less. Unemployed white high school graduates are twenty percentage points more likely to get a new job than black high school graduates—77.2% compared to 57.3%.

Younger workers are more mobile and move in and out of jobs more often than older workers, especially for less-educated white workers. Among white high school graduates, the probability that an unemployed worker returns to work is 77.2% for those between the ages of twenty and thirty, but only 59.4% for those thirty-one through forty.

The business cycle has its largest effects on the least educated. When unemployment is low, the likelihood that an unemployed high school dropout has returned to work two years later is 75.1% and 50.5%, respectively, for whites and blacks; these rates fall to 59.5% and 27.8%, respectively, when unemployment is high.

MONTHLY TRANSITIONS

The results presented thus far compare a man's employment status at one interview with his status at the interview two years later, ignoring

	HIGH SCHOOL DROPOUT	HIGH SCHOOL GRADUATE	SOME COLLEGE	COLLEGE GRADUATE
WHITE MALE BASELINE				
Baseline	68.5	77.2	72.5	88.8
Age 31–40	45.0	59.4	77.6	87.3
1970s	82.9	90.1	85.0	88.9
1980s	79.9	79.0	77.9	85.4
2001–2003	73.8	72.0	68.7	91.0
Min. unemployment (3.5)	75.1	83.3	83.7	87.9
Max. unemployment (9.7)	59.5	68.0	54.2	89.8
BLACK MALE BASELINE				
Baseline	39.6	57.3	65.8	*
Age 31–40	40.1	52.5	59.1	*
1970s	58.2	69.5	80.1	*
1980s	51.3	56.1	56.6	*
2001–2003	42.8	75.4	65.0	*
Min. unemployment (3.5)	50.5	54.3	71.1	*
Max. unemployment (9.7)	27.8	60.8	58.8	*

Source: Authors' calculations using PSID, 1970–2003. These use the specification from columns 2–5 of table 3.2 (estimated separately for whites and blacks) to predict exits to employment. Sample is restricted to male household heads, age 20–62, who were unemployed in the interview two years prior. Baseline individual is a male head of household between the ages of 20–30, in the 1990s with the mean unemployment rate over the 1968-2003 period. There are too few black college graduates in the PSID (about 38 per year) to make a meaningful prediction.

Table 3.4   Predicted likelihood of returning to work, male household heads

any transitions into and out of employment that occurred between interviews. In figure 3.7, we present monthly data, available in the PSID only from 1982 through 1999, to document transitions that occur during the two-year window for men who were employed at both the t-2 and t interviews. In the analyses above, these men were considered as not having experienced any employment instability.

The line with diamonds shows the fraction of men employed at both interviews who were unemployed at some point in the interim. This risk of unemployment fell dramatically, from 25% in the deepest recessionary year, 1982, to about 6% in the strongest boom year, 1999. This pattern is similar to the one shown in figure 3.5—between 1982 and 1999, the risk of moving from employment at interview t-2 to unemployment at t also fell.

The line with squares in figure 3.7 shows the fraction of men who switched employers during the two years between interviews without experiencing any unemployment. The fraction who switched jobs increased from about 8% over a two-year period in the early 1980s to about 15% in

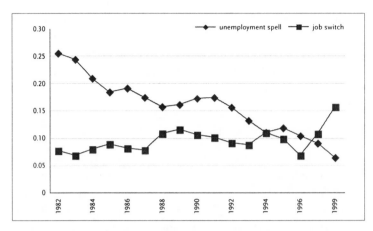

Figure 3.7   Likelihood of unemployment spell or job switch among male household heads employed in both year *t*-2 and year *t*   [Source: Authors' calculations using the PSID, 1968–2003]

1999. These results reflect the business cycle and are consistent with the declines in tenure with a single employer documented by Farber.[16]

When we estimate regressions using the 1982–1999 monthly data (not shown), the results are similar to those reported in table 3.1. The risk of experiencing any month of unemployment during a two-year period is higher for African Americans, for those with less education, and for younger workers.

We have analyzed changes in the risk of unemployment and the likelihood that the unemployed return to work using thirty-five years of panel data and documented that the labor market prospects of the disadvantaged worsened relative to those of more advantaged workers. Differences in trends in the employment rate and unemployment rate of low skilled and minority household heads are large. Among male heads of household between the ages of twenty and sixty-two, the gap between the employment rate of college graduates and that of high school dropouts was four percentage points in 1968, but rose to fifteen points in 2003. The racial employment gap also increased over these years from two to nine percentage points.

The risk of unemployment is higher for less-educated and black workers than for college graduates and white workers. The risk of unemployment rises and falls as the economy moves into and out of recessions. However, the risk, holding the unemployment rate constant, has increased in each decade from the 1970s to the present. Less educated and minority workers face a dual disadvantage in the labor market: they are more likely to lose a job and, at any unemployment rate, are less likely to find a new one.

NOTES

Acknowledgment: Rebecca Blank, Charles Brown, Brian Cadena, Peter Gottschalk, Katherine Newman, Robert Schoeni, and an anonymous referee provided helpful comments on a prior draft; David Ratner provided excellent research assistance. This project was supported in part by funds provided by the U.S. Department of Health and Human Services, Office of the Assistant Secretary for Planning and Evaluation, #5 UOI PE000001-05 and #I UOI AE000002-01. Any opinions and conclusions expressed are solely those of the authors and should not be construed as representing opinions or policy of any agency of the Federal government.

1   Rebecca M. Blank, Sheldon Danziger, and Robert Schoeni, "Work and Poverty During the Past Quarter Century," in *Working and Poor: How Economic and Policy Changes are Affecting Low-Wage Workers,* ed. Rebecca M. Blank, Sheldon Danziger. and Robert Schoeni (New York: Russell Sage Foundation, 2006), 1–20.

2   Richard B. Freeman, *America Works: Critical Thoughts on the Exceptional U.S. Labor Market* (New York: Russell Sage Foundation, 2007).

3   Related studies of employment security are also summarized in David Neumark, ed., *On the Job: Is Long-Term Employment a Thing of the Past?* (New York: Russell Sage Foundation, 2000), and Henry S. Farber, "Mobility and Stability: The Dynamics of Job Change in Labor Markets," in *Handbook of Labor Economics,* ed. Orley Ashenfelter and David Card (London: Elsevier Press, 1999), 2439–83.

4   Robert H. Topel and Michael P. Ward, "Job Mobility and the Careers of Young Men," *Quarterly Journal of Economics* 107, no. 2 (1992): 439–79.

5   Robert W. Fairlie and Lori G. Kletzer, "Jobs Lost, Jobs Regained: An Analysis of Black/White Differences in Job Displacement in the 1980s," *Industrial Relations* 37, no. 4 (1998): 460–77.

6   Francis X. Diebold, David Neumark, and Daniel Polsky, "Job Stability in the United States," *Journal of Labor Economics* 15, no. 2 (1997): 206–33.

7   Peter Gottschalk and Robert Moffitt, "Changes in Job Instability and Insecurity Using Monthly Survey Data," *Journal of Labor Economics* 17, no. 4 (1999): S91–S126.

8   Robert G. Valletta, "Declining Job Security," *Journal of Labor Economics* 17, no. 4 (1999): S170–S197. For analysis of patterns of involuntary job loss in the PSID, see

Johanne Boisjoly, Greg J. Duncan, and Timothy M. Smeeding, "The Shifting Incidence of Involuntary Job Losses from 1968 to 1992," *Industrial Relations* 37 (April 1998): 207–231.

9   Interviews were conducted annually between 1968 and 1997 and biennially after that date. As a result, we analyze the change in employment status over two-year periods between 1968 and 2003.

10 We do not evaluate work experiences between interviews. That is, some men who worked at both the t-2 and t interviews were unemployed at some time between these interviews, but are not counted as having exited to unemployment by our interview-to-interview method. For selected years, one can evaluate employment histories between interviews (see Gottschalk and Moffitt, "Changes in Job Instability"). For these years, we present results that are similar to the interview-to-interview results we discuss in the section "Monthly Transitions" beginning on p. 59.

11 See Valletta, "Declining Job Security."

12 Our sample includes men who are between the ages of twenty and sixty-two in each year. Thus, in each year of the thirty-five-year study period, men who were nineteen in the previous year enter the sample and those who were sixty-two age out of the sample. Because the new entrants have completed more years of schooling than the older workers exiting the sample, the average education of the sample and of the workforce increases over time. For example, high school dropouts were 39% of our sample in 1968, but only 13% in 2003; college graduates increased from 15% to 29% of the sample over these years. Thus, while we document that the relative risk of unemployment has increased more for high school dropouts than for more-educated workers, the reader should note that dropouts now represent a much smaller share of the workforce than they did in 1968.

13 These male employment-rate trends in the PSID are similar to those in the Current Population Survey. For example, between 1970 and 1999, among white men between the ages of twenty-five and fifty-four, the employment rate fell by seventeen percentage points for high school dropouts and by five points for men with at least a high school degree, but not a college degree (data not shown; provided to the authors by Deborah Reed, Public Policy Institute of California).

14 We estimate logistic regressions for male household heads in which the dependent variable is 1 if a worker at the time of the t-2 interview was unemployed when interviewed two years later. Coefficients are presented as log-odds ratios.

15 The first (t-2) year in the PSID is 1968, so the first t year in the tables is 1970.

16 See Chapter 1 in this volume. We have estimated regression models similar to those in tables 3.1 and 3.2 that utilize the monthly work history data that are available for the 1982–1999 period. Results are available on request from the authors.

CHAPTER FOUR

Rising Angst? | *Change and Stability in Perceptions of Economic Insecurity*

ELISABETH JACOBS & KATHERINE S. NEWMAN

"Free agency is over. Layoffs are back. Many of the people losing their jobs
are white collar and college educated. You could be next."

—*Fortune*, July 9, 2001

While scholars disagree over whether "real" insecurity has increased,
Americans' *experience* of their economic well-being remains a separate
question. Perceptions of risk and insecurity may or may not match real-
ity. The popular perception, for the moment, is that we have become a
worried nation. Magazines that usually trumpet the virtues of the market
have begun to point to the dark side. "The belief that stable jobs would
deliver steadily improving living standards has long been one of the major
REM cycles of the American dream," notes *Fortune* magazine. "But today
a queasy sense of insecurity haunts many working people. From neatly
coifed executives to aproned production workers, once secure futures
now seem threatened. Wave after wave of corporate restructurings has
knocked away the underpinnings of career-long employment that sustained workers' confidence in their future."[1] Is *Fortune* right? Have we
become motion-sick over declining fortunes?

In this chapter, we take a look at whether Americans are more
worried today about their economic futures than in the past, and which
groups of Americans express the greatest degrees of concern. We then
ask *why* these economic worries matters, and argue that the combination
of economic insecurity and economic inequality have real consequences

for public expectations and policy preferences. Here we focus on two particular issues: tolerance for inequality in general and, a related conviction, support for increasing government intervention to shore up the safety net that arguably protects workers and families from the vagaries of the market. We leave the question of the role these issues play in shifting or cementing partisan preferences to Philipp Rehm, whose chapter on that topic follows.

It is important to start with the most basic question this chapter poses: Are we actually more concerned about economic insecurity than we were in the past? The answer: It depends on the time horizon we pick and the groups we point to. There can be little question that we are an anxious nation today. But looking backward, over the period 1970–2000, we are actually a bit more optimistic than we used to be, at least in aggregate. Of course, aggregates don't tell us everything we want to know. In particular, they don't pinpoint which groups feel more uncertain, more vulnerable, and which have come to consider a certain level of insecurity "business as usual."

When we take the lens down to groups defined by income, education, or occupation, we find that there are different Americas out there, each with its own understanding of what the future holds economically. Those with less than a high school degree, for example, have long had to worry about their year-to-year economic stability. And their perceptions of economic security over time reflect this constant stress: they were worried before, and they're still worried today. But others — college graduates and white-collar professionals, for example — have developed motion sickness only in recent years.

AN ANXIOUS NATION?

Political analyst Ruy Teixeira recently observed that America is a "nation of unhappy campers," citing a 2005 Hart Research Associates/AFL-CIO poll that finds 54% of Americans are "worried and concerned" about reaching their economic goals (as compared to 43% who are "hopeful and confident").[2] The largest source of dissatisfaction is declining real wages and the resulting reduced standard of living: 53% of workers say that their incomes are not keeping up with prices, and 64% of workers worry "very or somewhat often" about prices rising faster than income.

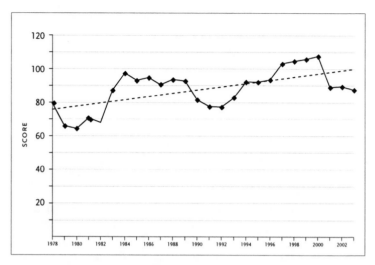

Figure 4.1   Index of consumer sentiment, 1978–2003

[Source: University of Michigan Survey of Consumers]

These concerns are widespread and seem to affect just about every group: college graduates, high school graduates, white-collar workers, and blue-collar workers. Over 75% of Americans are both dissatisfied with the country's economic situation *and* worried about achieving their economic and financial goals. A substantial majority of workers (63%) believe that in today's economy, it is hard to find "a good job with financial security even with a college degree."[3] A Lake Research Partners poll conducted in spring 2007 reports that 74% of American workers surveyed believe the American Dream is becoming harder to achieve, and over 80% agree that "no matter what you hear about the economy, working families are falling behind."[4]

The picture changes substantially, however, when we extend the time horizon and focus on long-term trends. The University of Michigan Index of Consumer Sentiment combines individuals' reports on their personal financial experience over the last year, their expectations for next year, and their perception of the national economic climate. The index scores range from a high of 108 (in 2000) to a low of 64 (in 1980). While scores have slipped since their historic peak in 2000, the overall trend since the beginning of data collection in 1978 is upward, which suggests we see ourselves as more secure—not less (figure 4.1).

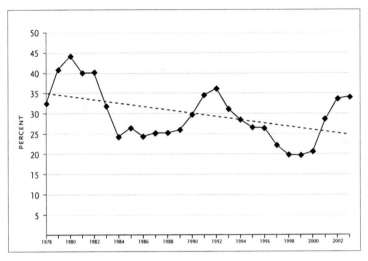

Figure 4.2 'I am in worse financial shape this year than last,' 1978–2003
[Source: University of Michigan Survey of Consumers]

The individual indicators that comprise the Index of Consumer Sentiment tell a similar story. For example, while the percent of Americans reporting that they are in worse financial shape this year than last has crept up in the last four years, fewer feel that way now than was the case over the period 1970–2000 (figure 4.2).

Other surveys confirm these findings. The National Opinion Research Center's General Social Survey (GSS) asks respondents to rate the likelihood that they will lose their jobs in the year to come. The percent reporting that they were "somewhat likely" or "likely" to be laid off or fired spiked in the early 1980s, 1990s, and post-2001, but the overall time trend since 1977 is virtually flat. On average, then, it would seem that Americans are not any more plagued by concern over job security today than they were in the past. While nearly 50% of all Americans reported to the GSS in 2004 that "finding an equivalent job would be hard," the data does not suggest a significant time trend (figure 4.3).

THREE AMERICAS?

Before we fold our tent and conclude that all is well—or at least that it is as well as it has ever been—we must examine exactly who has changed

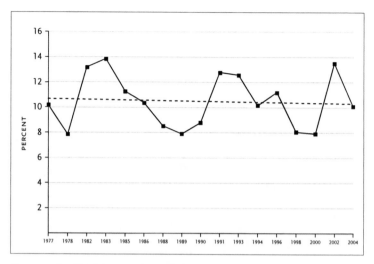

Figure 4.3 'I will likely lose my job next year,' 1977–2004
[Source: Authors' calculation from the General Social Survey]

and who has remained constant in their estimation of economic insecurity. When we dissect the overall trends, decomposing them into groups that differ in income, education, and occupation, we see the commonalities fade and the differences emerge (table 4.1).[5]

Let's start with income. Americans at the bottom of the income distribution are most likely to think that they are vulnerable to employment and financial insecurity: their views of their personal situation have changed very little since the 1970s. Low-income Americans are not only the most likely to believe they are likely to lose their jobs next year, but also the most likely to report that they are doing worse financially this year than last. As we move up the income ladder, insecurity over employment and financial well-being diminish steadily. The one area of economic angst that appears to impact all income groups equally is that of finding an equivalent job: on average over the past three decades, about 40% of respondents in all economic groups report that it would be hard to find a job with equivalent pay and benefits to their current job. In short: while (surprisingly large) portions of each tier of the economic distribution are haunted by the specter of insecurity, those at the bottom of the heap bear the greatest burden of worry.

	JOB LOSS LIKELY	FINDING EQUIVALENT JOB HARD	FINANCIAL SITUATION WORSE THIS YEAR
INCOME			
Bottom 25%	18.43	40.55	31.41
Lower-middle	12.11	40.62	22.46
Upper-middle	8.64	41.38	17.41
Top 25%	6.86	39.71	15.34
EDUCATION			
Less than high school	15.32	51.24	25.95
High school	11.57	42.32	21.76
College	6.58	33.08	16.35
OCCUPATION			
Operator/craftsmen	15.40	47.78	23.62
Clerical worker	11.19	45.29	21.57
Service worker	11.42	35.58	24.91
Professional/ technical worker	6.40	34.08	17.15
Manager	7.02	38.57	18.86

Table 4.1   Average levels of perceived economic insecurity

[Source: Authors' calculations from the General Social Survey, 1972–2004]

Education matters as well. The least educated Americans are today—and have been since the late 1970s—far more economically insecure than their better-educated peers. Americans with less than a high school education are the most likely to report significant employment and financial anxiety. Not only are they more likely than their more-educated peers to believe that their jobs will be at risk within the next year, they are more likely than others to believe that finding an equivalent job would be difficult. The least educated also report a greater degree of deterioration in their overall financial situation over the last year. As we travel up the education ladder, employment and financial anxiety steadily diminish. While college-educated Americans have always been more secure, on average, than their less-educated peers, they too experience significant levels of anxiety. For example, 33% of college-educated Americans report that finding an equivalent job would be difficult, and 16% report that their economic situation this year was worse than last year. This is not to say that college grads are unconcerned about their finances and employment prospects; it is only to say—consistent with what human capital theory would predict—that they are less worried than those who have fewer credentials to put on the table.

Along with income and education, occupational differences predict varying levels of economic insecurity. Given the long, slow erosion of American manufacturing, it is not particularly surprising that "operators and craftsmen" perceive the greatest degree of economic risk. The industries within which they are employed have been hammered by globalization, which shows no signs of abating, and they correctly perceive that these macro conditions have negative personal consequences for their security.[6] Clerical and service workers are marginally more secure, while professional and technical workers and managers enjoy the highest levels of security. While 15% of operators and craftsmen believe job loss next year was likely, only 7% of managers worried about losing their jobs. Similar differences between occupational groups exist for perceived difficulty of finding an equivalent job, and for the percent reporting a worse financial situation this year than last. White-collar workers, in general, feel more secure in their economic position than do their blue- and pink-collar peers.

WEAKNESS IN THE WINNER'S CIRCLE

These variations between groups—by education, income, and occupation—have persisted over the last three decades. But while some have held steady in their perceptions, others have seen their worries grow—sharply. Surprisingly, again given human capital advantages, the change for the worse has been most pronounced for the group we might expect to be most secure: the economic winners, college-educated Americans and managers.

When asked whether they are likely to lose their jobs in the next year, an increasing proportion of college graduates have answered "yes" over the last thirty years (figure 4.4). They have become somewhat more optimistic about the potential for finding an equivalent job, despite a recent spike in concern (figure 4.5), but the same cannot be said for financial well-being. The proportion who say they did worse financially this year than last has crept upward (figure 4.6). Although a college education provides a more reliable security blanket than those with less education

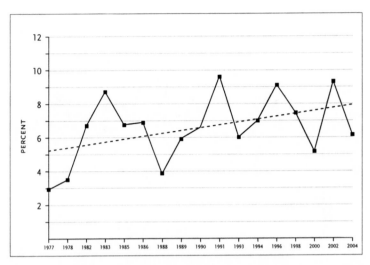

Figure 4.4 'I will likely lose my job next year' (college graduates), 1977–2004
[Source: Authors' calculations from the General Social Survey]

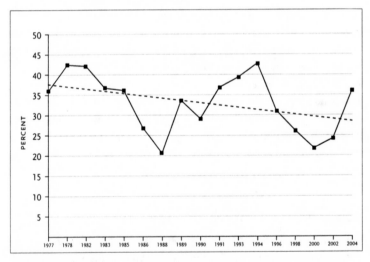

Figure 4.5 'Finding an equivalent job would be hard' (college graduates), 1977–2004
[Source: Authors' calcuations from the General Social Survey]

can hope to have, it is becoming more threadbare as the years go by.

American managers are less likely to be happy campers as well. Since the late 1970s, managerial workers have increasingly reported that

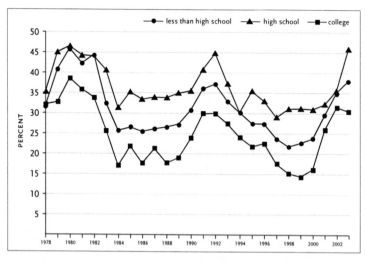

Figure 4.6   'I am in worse financial shape this year than last' (by education), 1978–2003
[Source: Michigan Survey of Consumer Behavior]

they worry they will lose their jobs in the year to come. Particularly bad years were 1991 and 2002 — nearly 16% of all managers reported likely job loss in both (figure 4.7). They don't seem to have changed in their sense of how easy it will be to find an equivalent new job (figure 4.8), but they have definitely seen a decline in their financial security, with 1989 and 2002 standing out as bad years (figure 4.9). Nearly 35% of all managers reported that they did worse financially this year than last in both of these years. In general, the percentage of American managers who report doing worse financially this year than last has increased over the last three decades.

SQUARING PERCEPTIONS WITH "REALITY"

Do Americans have it right? Are their expectations for economic or employment security "on the money" or wide of the mark? A quick review of the data on income and employment suggests that they have a pretty good fix on the situation.

Anne Huff Stevens and Henry S. Farber have debated this issue with respect to long-term job tenure in earlier chapters in this volume.[7] Here we focus on another measure of job insecurity: the displacement

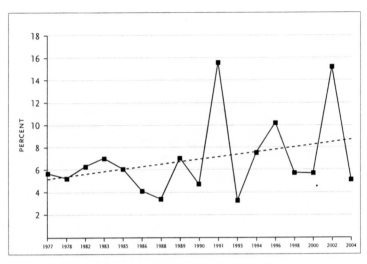

Figure 4.7 'I will likely lose my job next year '(managers), 1977–2004
[Source: Authors' calcuation from the General Social Survey]

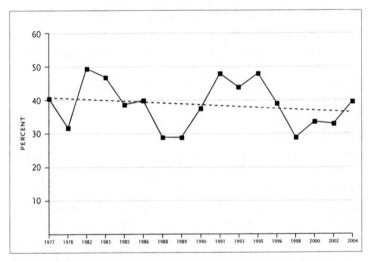

Figure 4.8 'Finding an equivalent job would be hard' (managers), 1977–2004
[Source: Authors' calculation from the General Social Survey]

rate, or, in simple terms, the probability that a worker would lose a job due to no fault of his or her own. The displacement rate is, intuitively, countercyclic. When the economy grows, involuntary job loss is less

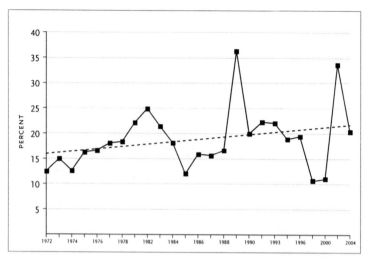

Figure 4.9 'I am in worse financial shape this year than last' (managers), 1972–2004
[Source: Authors' calculation from the General Social Survey]

common than when the economy contracts. Overall, job insecurity in the halcyon days of the late 1990s was relatively low, clocking in at about the same level as in the economic boom of the late 1980s. The endurance of a countercyclical displacement rate suggests that, in the aggregate, the probability of involuntary displacement today is just as dependent on economic growth as it always has been. In short: Job insecurity is no more or less common today than it was in the past.[8]

But what past are we measuring today's experience against? To argue that job security today is on a par with the 1980s may be setting a low bar. Indeed, Johanne Boisjoly, Greg J. Duncan, and Timothy M. Smeeding find that 1980 was a critical tipping point for rates of involuntary job loss, with displacement rates substantially lower prior to 1980.[9] Both the pre-1980 and post-1980 periods that Boisjoly and his team analyze include two substantial economic downturns, hence their results suggest that a structural shift toward a more volatile economy occurred some time around 1980.

Although involuntary job loss may not be on the rise, the consequences of job loss have shifted in fundamental ways over time, particularly for older workers. The costs of job loss have always been substantial, but they are more consequential today than in the recent past. Displaced workers are now somewhat more likely to find a new job, but the quality of that job typically differs markedly from their former position. Those who take new positions following the loss of a job suffer a significant pay cut. Apart from the welcome spike that we saw in the boom years of the late 1990s, reemployed workers have endured weekly earnings losses of at least 10% since the 1980s, with the most recent data (from 2001) suggesting even deeper cuts.[10] Older workers today face particularly steep challenges following job displacement. Two years after a job loss at age fifty-five, just 60% of men and 55% of women were employed, compared with a rate of more than 80% among nondisplaced men and women who were working at age fifty-five. Even four years after displacement, there was a 20% gap between the displaced and nondisplaced groups' employment rates.[11]

It is also important to note that the early 1980s marked a fundamental shift in who experienced displacement. As Katherine Newman observed in *Falling From Grace: Downward Mobility in the Age of Affluence*, the early 1980s marked the first time that white-collar managerial workers experienced displacement in large numbers.[12] Between the end of World War II and the deep recession of the early Reagan years, these highly educated and experienced workers were reasonably well-protected; for blue-collar workers, displacement was a fact of life. Layoffs, seasonal closures, and — in good years — callbacks when the factories reopened was a common pattern, even though it produced hardship for working-class families.

This was not the experience or the expectation of the best-educated American workers, but in the early 1980s, downsizing and outsourcing began to impact this group as well and their displacement rates shot up. As such, comparing the present to the 1980s once again captures an economic experience that had already departed sharply from the more tranquil past.[13] The rate of job loss among America's most educated — those with a college degree (or at least sixteen years of education) — has increased more steeply than the rate of job loss among the less educated. By 2001, job loss among the most educated was at a twenty-year high of 11%. Reemployment for college-educated Americans has become more and more difficult, and the post-1990s bust appears to have hit this group particularly hard. In addition, college-educated job losers face the steepest financial penalties. The earnings losses associated with taking a new job following unemployment have risen substantially

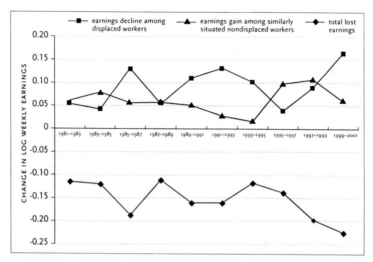

Figure 4.10 Total lost earnings amongst displaced college-educated workers, 1983–2001

[Source: Calculations by Henry Farber from the Displaced Worker Survey; see note 8]

over the last few decades, with those losses coming from two different sources. First, displaced workers face declining earnings. Second, the earnings of similarly-situated individuals who were fortunate enough to remain employed continue to rise over the same period that displaced workers' earnings fall. If we compare a displaced worker's earnings post-displacement to what she would have been earning had she not lost her job, we see a steady drop in the fortunes of displaced college-educated workers beginning in the mid-1990s. By 2001, a college-educated worker could expect to lose about 23% of her earnings following the loss of a job (figure 4.10).[14]

It would seem that the different groups we have examined have a pretty good handle on these changes, given the "facts on the ground." The relative optimism of higher-income Americans as compared to their lower-income peers makes sense. Between 1979 and 2004, incomes grew across the income distribution, but that growth was uneven. The top fifth of the income distribution saw much larger gains than any other quintile, and gains just of the top 1% dwarfed those of the top 5% (figure 4.11). As a result, the share of household income held by the top fifth of the income distribution has skyrocketed, while share of household income held by the bottom fifth of the distribution has actually decreased.[15] As

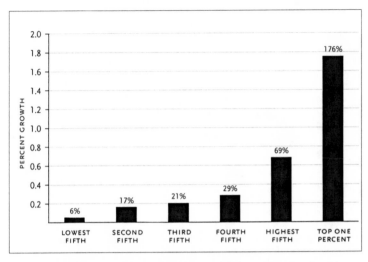

Figure 4.11   Growth in after-tax income by income quintile, 1979–2004
[Source: Congressional Budget Office]

such, the comparatively rosy perceptions of economic security among the wealthiest Americans mesh well with the aggregate economic trends. And the glum outlook of America's poor is on-target too.

The anxiety of less-educated workers as compared to their more-educated peers mirrors the graduated experiences of these groups in the labor market. The least educated are indeed the most likely to lose their jobs and the least likely to be reemployed and that has been the norm over the last two decades (figures 4.12, 4.13). The toll suffered by displaced workers is somewhat different, however. In the 1980s, the least educated unemployed fared worst, suffering greater proportional losses to their earnings upon reemployment than their more-educated counterparts. By the 1990s, however, this situation had reversed. Upon reemployment, the least educated workers now lose less than their better-educated peers (figure 4.14).[16] Of course, given the well-documented decline in the fortunes of America's least educated workers, it is probably the case that the jobs they are losing pay so poorly that they cannot fall very much farther down the ladder of income if they can find new jobs at all.[17] Losing a job flipping burgers and finding a new one as a parking lot attendant may not mean much of a pay cut, but it certainly doesn't mean things are looking up either.

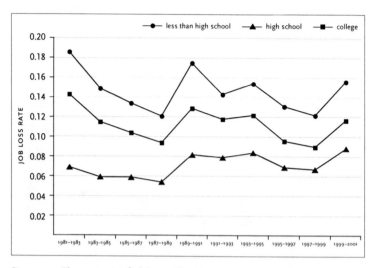

Figure 4.12   Three-year rate of job loss, 1983–2001

[Source: Calculations by Henry Farber from the Displaced Worker Survey; see note 8]

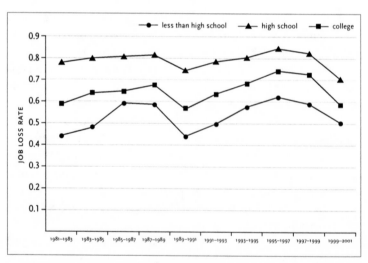

Figure 4.13   Percent of job losers employed at survey date, 1983–2001

[Source: Calculations by Henry Farber from the Displaced Worker Survey; see note 8]

Rising levels of insecurity among those who have "made it" suggest that the American Dream is under a lot of pressure. When college-educated Americans and managerial professionals express greater con-

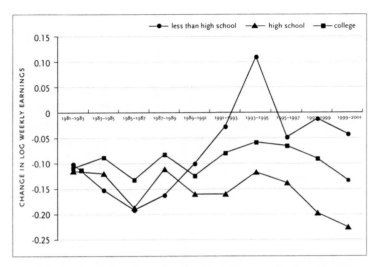

Figure 4.14 Change in weekly earnings earnings amongst displaced workers, 1983–2001
[Source: Calculations by Henry Farber from the Displaced Worker Survey; see note 8]

cern for their security, America listens. They vote. Moreover, the power of their voice is magnified by what they represent. If the most advantaged among us are lying awake at night, thinking about how to cover their bills or whether they will have a job next year, what hope is there for the millions of others who lack their credentials and savings accounts?

CONSEQUENCES FOR THE SOCIAL COMPACT

The perception of income and employment insecurity and the difficulty of recovering from job loss are not disconnected from the larger problem of growing inequality. As is well-known by now, income inequality in the United States is at the highest level we have experienced since the 1920s.[18] Average executive pay grew by nearly 300% between 1990 and 2005, as compared to just over a 4% growth in pay for the average worker during that time.[19] Well-educated managers who are feeling the tremors of job insecurity sit well below the vaunted station of CEOs, and many of those managers have felt the fallout from outsourcing in the form of a thinning of the ranks in middle management.[20] Nonetheless, they were far better protected than the blue-collar workers who, as we've shown, accurately recognize their persistent vulnerability.

Some have argued that the growth in economic inequality has occurred because of rising popular acceptance of wide income gaps. Most notably, in a 2002 article for the *New York Times Magazine*, Paul Krugman argues that the standard accounts—globalization, skills-biased technological change, and the winner-take-all hypothesis—do not fully explain the trend.[21] Globalization could explain part of the decline in the median wage, but it couldn't explain the explosive growth in CEO pay. Technology might explain why the premium associated with a college education increased, but does not help us make sense of the growth in inequality among the college educated. And the winner-take-all theory might explain Michael Jordan's phenomenal wealth, but what of all those billionaires who can't dunk? Perhaps, wondered Krugman, social norms were at the heart of the matter:

> Some—by no means all—economists trying to understand growing inequality have begun to take seriously a hypothesis that would have been considered irredeemably fuzzy-minded not long ago. This view stresses the role of social norms in setting limits to inequality. According to this view, the New Deal had a more profound impact on American society than even its most ardent admirers have suggested: it imposed norms of relative equality in pay that persisted for more than thirty years, creating the broadly middle-class society we came to take for granted. But those norms began to unravel in the 1970s and have done so at an accelerating pace.[22]

Is Krugman right? Have the social norms bolstering the society that produced the New Deal and the Great Society unraveled over the last thirty years? Alongside a normalization of insecurity—now most pronounced among blue-collar workers and nervously eyed by managers and executives—are we seeing a sobering recognition or acceptance of the unequal status quo?

In this section, we provide evidence contrary to Krugman's thesis. Far from tolerating the widening gap between haves and have-nots, Americans express frustration with the levels of economic inequality that they perceive and experience first-hand in the form of job and financial instability. And their policy preferences fall in line with the norms we might expect under these conditions. Indeed, despite the public perception that we have become an increasingly conservative country (especially relative to our European counterparts)—as evidence by the tough welfare reform bill of 1996—support for redistributive social programs and safety-net spending has actually ticked upward over this period. While the public maintains its strong preferences for government spending targeting working people and the middle class as compared to the poor and those on welfare, support for all social programs has grown modestly in the last several decades. We interpret this data as reflective of frustration with the inegalitarian status quo. To be clear, it's not that Americans have become more generous over time. We see little evidence for a sharp lurch in the progressive direction. Instead, we see that basic sensibilities of fairness are stretched to the limit, and mildly greater support for politics that would level the playing field are more evident in public opinion data.

Frustration with economic polarization is clear in the General Social Survey's Social Inequality module (GSS–SI), a set of questions tapping attitudes toward economic polarization, and fielded three times: 1987, 1992, and 1999. The percent of respondents saying they were very concerned with income inequality rose from 59% in 1987 to 66% in 1999. Similarly, the percent expressing grave concern over wage inequality rose from 37% in 1987 to 69% in 1999 (table 4.2).

These findings suggest a fundamental weakness in the social norms explanation of rising inequality, and call into question whether the social compact has indeed "unraveled." As economic fortunes diverge, everyday Americans express increasing concern with the cleavages. These figures do not suggest that we are less tolerant of inequality, in an absolute sense, than we were in earlier periods. Increasing levels of frustration with economic inequality track closely with increasing *real* inequality. This dual trend suggests that Americans' tolerance for inequality may not have changed, but that the level of inequality the country has experienced over the last several decades has exceeded what Americans are willing to accept.[23]

Krugman and others argue that the "Greatest Generation"—which came of age during the New Deal—was less tolerant of economic inequality than the generations that followed.[24] As these elders pass away and are replaced by succeeding generations that are more accepting of inequality, are we seeing exploding wage growth at the top? In short: no. When we break the GSS-SI data into birth cohorts, we find little consistent variation between them. For the death of the Greatest Generation to have a causal impact on attitudes toward inequality, we should see markedly more

	1987	1992	1999	TOTAL	1987–1992	1992–1999	1987–1999
CONTINUOUS MEASURES	MEANS (STANDARD DEVIATIONS)				CHANGES IN MEANS/ STANDARD DEVIATIONS		
Income inequality too high	3.53 (1.04)	3.92 (0.96)	3.77 (1.03)	3.73 (1.03)	0.38	0.15	0.23
Wage inequality too high	-0.29 (1.04)	-0.10 (1.08)	0.17 (1.13)	-0.08 (1.09)	0.17	0.25	0.42
DICHOTOMOUS MEASURES	PERCENT				PERCENT CHANGE		
Income inequality: most concerned	59.06	77.17	66.46	67.06	30.66	-13.88	12.53
Wage inequality: most concerned	37.17	45.78	69.22	50.55	33.16	51.20	86.23

All cross-time means differences are significant at $p \le .10$. Income Inequality Too High ranges from 1 to 5. Wage Inequality Too High ranges from -6.16 to 4.74. In both cases, higher values represent more egalitarian responses. Income Inequality Too High: Agree is a dichotomous variable coded 1 for all individuals with either Agree or Strongly Agree responses on Income Inequality Too High. Wage Inequality Too High: Agree is a dichotomous variable coded 1 for all individuals with positive scores on Wage Inequality Too High. Data are from the ISSP Social Inequality Modules I, II, and III. United States sub-sample of the ISSP Social Inequality Modules I, II, and III. (N = 2594).

Table 4.2   Public tolerance for economic inequality in the United States, 1987–1999
[Source: Authors' calculations from the General Social Survey]

egalitarian tendencies among them as compared to their children and their children's children. Ironically, the reverse seems to be the case. The Greatest Generation is the least concerned about wage inequality of the five cohort groups. As such, nothing in the empirical evidence suggests that generational replacement is driving economic trends (table 4.3).

The data suggest that contemporary levels of inequality have surpassed Americans' comfort zone, but what of our policy preferences? In a previous work, we suggested that as far back as the New Deal, Americans were more likely to embrace a social safety net for workers than they were for those who were out of the labor force.[25] Even in the Great Depression, public opinion ran against the earliest form of welfare. Is that still the case?

The country's commitment to social welfare policy has endured. Over the period in which inequality has grown, respondents express greater approval of the role government plays in redistributing income from high- to low-income Americans, and from the rich to the poor.

	COHORT 1 b. 1930–44	COHORT 2 b. 1945–54	COHORT 3 b. 1955–69	COHORT 4 b. 1970–83	1992	1999
OLS MODELS (BETA COEFFICIENTS)						
Income inequality	-0.017	-0.01	-0.075	-0.189	0.427**	0.163**
	0.17	0.12	0.15	0.15	0.01	0.01
Wage inequality	0.254*	0.327**	0.295+	0.161	0.192**	0.412**
	0.06	0.04	0.09	0.15	0.01	0.01
LOGIT MODELS (ODDS RATIOS)						
Income inequality:	0.805	0.83	0.753	0.542+	2.548**	1.139**
most concerned	0.22	0.15	0.25	0.2	0.08	0.02
Wage inequality:	1.374+	1.279*	1.437*	1.14	1.445**	3.604**
most concerned	0.25	0.16	0.24	0.31	0.02	0.12

Robust standard errors in italics. Reference categories are Cohort 1 (b. 1905–29) and 1987. In addition to birth cohort and year, models control for income, education, subjective social class, gender, labor status (unemployed or self-employed), union membership, and skill-specificity. Data are from the United States subsample of the ISSP Social Inequality Modules I, II, and III. (N = 2594). + significant at 10% * significant at 5% ** significant at 1%

Table 4.3   Cohort as predictor of attitudes toward inequality in the United States, 1987–1999
[Source: Authors' calculations from the General Social Survey]

Safety-net expenditures, particularly unemployment and retirement spending, are endorsed more strongly (table 4.4).[26] Our interpretation of this bump in support for safety-net spending mirrors our explanation for the increase in frustration with inequality and the increasingly bumpy road Americans experience even at the high end of the educational and occupational spectrum. As the safety net has unraveled and inequality has grown, Americans express more support for spending in relation to a status quo that they perceive as inadequate.

The General Social Survey is not the only data source to reflect these trends. The same modest positive trajectory is evident in the National Election Studies (NES). While the GSS data allows us to get a sense of trends through the early 1990s, the NES data gives us a more detailed picture of trends over the most recent ten years, from 1992 to 2002. It shows us that support for social welfare spending was on the rise, with the exception of a dip between 1994 and 1996, a period of Republican ascendance in Congress. Support for federal spending on the poor was at its nadir in 1996, but steadily increased over the next eight years. Similarly, support for federal welfare spending bottomed out in 1996 and then steadily climbed to a ten-year high in 2002 (table 4.5). As with the

	1985	1990	1996	TOTAL	1985–1990	1990–1996	1985–1996
	MEANS (STANDARD DEVIATIONS)				CHANGES IN MEANS/ STANDARD DEVIATIONS		
GOVERNMENT SHOULD REDUCE INCOME DIFFERENCES...							
Between high/ low incomes	2.21 (1.1)	2.36 (1.04)	2.4 (1.05)	2.34 (1.06)	0.14	0.04	0.18
Between rich/poor	2.73 (1.3)	2.92 (1.15)	2.83 (1.29)	2.85 (1.24)	0.15	-0.07	0.08
GOVERNMENT SPENDING SHOULD BE INCREASED FOR...							
Health care	3.62 (0.85)	3.89 (0.77)	3.77 (0.86)	3.78 (0.83)	0.33	-0.14	0.18
Retirement	3.4 (0.94)	3.49 (0.89)	3.52 (0.89)	3.48 (0.9)	0.1	0.03	0.13
Unemployment	3.02 (0.99)	3.07 (0.94)	3.09 (0.93)	3.07 (0.95)	0.05	0.02	0.07

All cross-time means differences are significant at p ≤ .10. Variables range from 1 to 5, with 5 representing the strongest preferences for spending. Data are from the ISSP Role of Government Modules I, II, and III. (N = 3224).

Table 4.4   Changes in preference for government redistribution and social safety net spending, 1985–1996   [Source: Authors' calculations from the General Social Survey]

GSS trends, we view these data as suggestive of fixed safety-net spending preferences. Public opinion on spending tracks perceptions of the status quo—when inequality is perceived to be too high and spending is perceived to be low, spending preferences reflect this dissatisfaction.[27]

The NES provides additional evidence suggestive of stable attitudes toward both the poor and welfare recipients. For most years between 1976 and 2004, the NES has asked respondents to rate on a "thermometer" calibrated from zero to one hundred their feelings toward welfare recipients. Unlike questions asking whether spending is "too high" or "too low," thermometer questions do not contain implicit references to the status quo. As such, they offer a better "absolute" measure of Americans' sentiments toward the poor. Despite a few bumps, most notably a dip in the mid-1990s, thermometer ratings toward welfare recipients suggest stability rather than change. The cumulative change in attitudes is only 2.5% of the entire one hundred-point scale. Today's average American has more or less the same basic feelings toward welfare

	POOLED	1984	1986	1988	1990	1992	1994	1996	2000	2002
SPENDING	1.54	..	..	..	..	1.52	..	1.62	1.55	1.49
ON POOR	0.64	..	..	..	..	0.62	..	0.68	0.65	0.61
WELFARE	2.26	..	..	..	..	2.25	2.4	2.43	2.21	2.05
	0.73	..	..	..	..	0.73	0.72	0.7	0.71	0.51
FOOD	2.16	2.11	2.06	2.1	2.09	2.12	2.32	2.35	2.16	..
STAMPS	0.7	0.73	0.75	0.73	0.64	0.68	0.65	0.67	0.68	..
SOCIAL	1.46	1.52	1.38	1.44	1.4	1.56	1.51	1.56	1.4	1.39
SECURITY	0.57	0.57	0.55	0.55	0.55	0.58	0.59	0.61	0.57	0.54

Standard deviations are italicized. Spending preferences are coded categorically: 1=Increase, 2=Keep Same, 3=Decrease. Note that lower values indicate stronger support.

Table 4.5   Federal spending preferences, 1984–2002

[Source: Authors' calculations from the National Election Studies Cumulative Data File]

recipients as did her peer during the Great Society. We interpret this data as an indication of basic stability in attitudes toward America's poor.[28]

Welfare was a hot-button topic throughout the 1980s and 1990s. As Cybelle Fox notes, "the political rhetoric and media images that surround the public debate about welfare have often been inflammatory, derogatory, and racially coded."[29] That public opinion of welfare, welfare recipients, and the poor dipped in the mid-1990s is clear. In the decade since, however, public opinion toward welfare seems to have rebounded (figure 4.15). The patterns in the NES data suggest that attributing the mid-1990s dip to broad, permanent changes in social norms is a mistake. Public opinion seems to have responded to elite attention to the policy issue—President Clinton's campaign promises to "end welfare as we know it" in 1992, and the congressional Republicans' 1994 Contract with America, to give two examples.

We should note, as well, that the popularity of "sacred" spending programs like Social Security also took a hit during the mid-1990s and similarly bounced back between 1996 and 2004 (table 4.5). It would appear that the mid-1990s was a period of overarching frustration with government in general. In the years following 1996, American attitudes toward social welfare and social insurance spending have enjoyed a rebound that has endured both the booming economy of the late 1990s and the post-9/11 economic downturn.

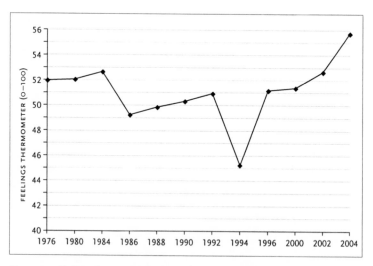

Figure 4.15   Feelings thermometer toward welfare recipients, 1976–2004
[Source: National Election Studies Cumulative Data File]

In short, the contemporary period has been a time of neither rising tolerance for inequality nor declining support for the social safety net. Public opinion on a host of safety net policies, ranging from health care to welfare to unemployment to Social Security to general spending on the poor all reflect a basic stability in generosity over the last two decades, with the exception of the dip in the mid-1990s.

This is not to say that the United States has become Sweden. While warmth toward welfare recipients may not have eroded over the last twenty years, it remains well below that toward the middle class: on a thermometer feelings scale, welfare recipients score a mean of fifty-one degrees while middle-class Americans score a mean of seventy-five degrees (table 4.6, figure 4.16).[30] Support for Social Security spending, a program grounded in work and individual responsibility, has remained substantially higher than support for welfare or food stamps spending (table 4.5).

The promise of opportunity and upward mobility has long been a bedrock expectation in the United States. In general, that optimism has stayed

	POOLED	1972	1974	1976	1980	1984	1986	1988
Middle class	74.85	73.59	77.57	73.95	75.61	72.55	..	..
	16.45	*16.77*	*15.99*	*15.73*	*16.26*	*17.04*	..	..
Poor people	71.84	73.14	76.57	71.13	74.55	71.25	72.64	68.87
	18.38	*16.96*	*17.47*	*17.31*	*17.61*	*18.34*	*18.66*	*18.75*
Welfare recipients	50.87	..	..	51.97	52.05	52.66	49.23	49.85
	21.63	..	..	*20.96*	*22.79*	*21.42*	*23.12*	*21.03*

	1990	1992	1994	1996	1998	2000	2002	2004
Middle class	..	..	..	..	..	..	..	76.17
	..	..	..	..	..	..	..	*16.65*
Poor people	75.54	70.15	71.15	70.38	70.78	69.64	65.4	72.77
	18.85	*17.29*	*18.96*	*17.39*	*19.48*	*19.62*	*19.12*	*18.52*
Welfare recipients	50.32	50.94	45.23	51.18		51.39	52.67	55.73
	24.13	*19.73*	*23.51*	*19.77*		*20.52*	*19.42*	*19.9*

Standard deviations are italicized. Feelings thermometer runs from cold (o degrees) to warm (100 degrees).

Table 4.6   Feelings thermometer temperatures from the national election study, 1972–2004
[Source: Authors' calculations from the National Election Studies Cumulative Data File]

with us over time. Yet underneath the optimistic gloss lie the demons of risk and the potential for a tumble down the rungs of the economic ladder. Those at the bottom of the ladder have always been the most concerned about their economic stability—the sizable percentage of lower-income and less-well-educated Americans who report ill-ease over their job stability, their prospects for reemployment, and their economic well-being this year as compared to last all suggest that the American Dream rings hollow for some. Sadly, they have long had to contend with the insecurity that comes with a less-stable job market and the weaker credentials they bring to the table in an economy that rewards the highly educated to a much greater extent.

Yet it is upper echelon Americans —highly-educated Americans with white-collar, managerial jobs —who register the greatest change in the direction of anxiety over their futures, and not without reason. Though comparatively well positioned, they have seen the greatest erosion in their prospects, at least as far as their expectations for durable employment and their financial stability year to year.

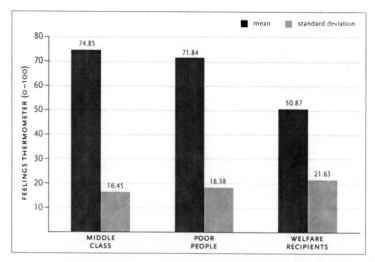

Figure 4.16   Differences in attitudes toward the middle class, the poor, and welfare recipients, 1972–2004   [Source: National Election Studies Cumulative Data File]

These sources of anxiety may well be fueling the discontent we have traced over widening income inequality. If everyone is getting richer or enjoying the pleasures of a stable labor market, then the fact that some are rocketing into the stratosphere in income terms may be less problematic. Instead, the growing gap between those at the top and the rest of us is creating discontent. The idea that the top fraction is pulling away from the rest of society is not acceptable to most Americans and is becoming less so as the gaps open up. The change cannot be explained by the change of generations. Today's adults are, if anything, more disturbed by growing inequality than their predecessors in the Greatest Generation.

It has been suggested that equal frustration is experienced by Americans as they cast their eyes down the ladder of social stratification.[31] Particularly in times of economic strife, do middle-class Americans place blame on those less fortunate than themselves? Negative sentiment toward welfare recipients and declining support for government intervention in the form of a meaningful safety net might be expected under these circumstances, particularly given the long period of Republican domination of the White House. Yet the data show a constant—though not especially warm—"temperature" toward welfare recipients and consistent, even modestly increased, enthusiasm for the social safety net, especially Social Security.

Again, in a period in which vulnerability is felt up and down the ladder, except at the very top, sustained support for the social compact seems to be more forthcoming than the policy dynamics of the period would suggest.

NOTES

Epigraph: Betsy Morris, "White Collar Blues," *Fortune*, July 9, 2001.

1 Louis Richman, "Getting Past Economic Insecurity," *Fortune*, April 17, 1995.

2 Ruy Teixeira, "Public Opinion Watch: Workers Are Unhappy Campers," *Mother Jones*, September 2, 2005.

3 Peter D. Hart Research Associates/AFL–CIO, "Labor Day 2005: The State of Working America," August 2005, http://www.aflcio.org/aboutus/laborday/upload/ld2005_report.pdf.

4 Lake Research Partners, "Anger, Anxiety and the American Dream," April 4, 2007, http://www.changetowin.org/fileadmin/pdf/executive_summary_poll_04042007.pdf.

5 We also find substantial difference between men and women's perceptions of economic security in the University of Michigan Survey of Consumers—women are consistently more anxious than men. The evidence of the gender difference in the General Social Survey is far less clear, however.

6 While the GSS allows us to investigate attitudes toward job security across various sociodemographic groups, it does not allow for an empirical analysis of the causes of these attitudes. For instance, the GSS does not allow for a direct test of whether some occupational groups feel more threatened than others due to the pressures of globalization. Although not in the scope of this chapter, future research on this topic could investigate the causal link between globalization's impact and attitudes toward job insecurity, perhaps by linking macroeconomic data on import pressure by occupation to GSS data on attitudes toward job insecurity.

7 In addition to Huff Stevens' and Farber's analysis of long-term job tenure, Federal Reserve economist Robert Valletta has contributed important research to the field. He finds that while average job security may have remained stable over time, the aggregate masks important trends for specific demographic groups. Valletta finds that aggregate job tenure has remained relatively stable because rising median job tenure for women has offset falling job tenure for men. Median job tenure for thirty-five- to fifty-year-old males, who comprise one-third of the total labor force, declined substantially between 1983 and 2006. See Robert Valletta, "Anxious Workers," Federal Reserve Bank of San Francisco *Economic Letter* 2007-13 (2007).

8   All trends and figures are drawn from Henry Farber, "Job Loss in the United States, 1981–2001," *National Bureau of Economic Research Working Papers*, no. 9797 (2003), http://www.nber.org/papers/w9707.

9   Johanne Boisjoly, Greg J. Duncan, and Timothy M. Smeeding, "The Changing Incidence of Involuntary Job Loss," *Industrial Relations* 37 (April 1998): 207–231.

10 All trends and figures are drawn from Farber, "Job Loss in the United States."

11 See Sewan Chan and Ann Huff Stevens,"Job Loss and Employment Patterns of Older Workers," *Journal of Labor Economics* 19 (2001): 484–521.

12 Katherine S. Newman, *Falling From Grace: Downward Mobility in the Age of Affluence* (Berkeley: University of California Press, 1999).

13 As noted above, an analysis of economic trends by occupation is outside of the scope of this chapter. We anticipate investigating this perception/reality matchup further in future work.

14 Figures are drawn from Farber, "Job Loss in the United States." For further discussion of the changing profile of displaced workers, see Daniel Rodriguez and Madeline Zavodny, "Changes in the Age and Education Profile of Displaced Workers," *Industrial and Labor Relations Review* 56 (2003): 498–510; Robert G. Valletta, "Declining Job Security," *Journal of Labor Economics* 17 (1999): s170–s197.

15 See Jared Bernstein, Lawrence Mishel, and Chauna Brocht, "Any Way You Cut It: Income Inequality on the Rise Regardless of How It's Measured," Economic Policy Institute, http://www.epi.org/content.cfm/briefingpapers_inequality_inequality.

16 Trends and figures are drawn from Farber, "Job Loss in the United States."

17 For a synthesis of the declining earning power of the least educated Americans, see David Card and John DiNardo, "Skill-Biased Technological Change and Rising Wage Inequality: Some Puzzles and Problems," *Journal of Labor Economics* 20 (2002): 733–83.

18 Thomas Piketty and Emanuel Saez, "Income Inequality in the United States, 1913–1998," *National Bureau of Economic Research Working Papers*, no. 8467 (2001), http://www.nber.org/papers/w8467.

19 See "CEO Pay, Stock Prices, Corporate Profits, Worker Pay, and Inflation, 1990–2005," United for a Fair Economy, http://www.faireconomy.org/research/CEO_Pay_charts.html. Average worker pay data are from the Bureau of Labor Statistics, and average CEO pay data are from survey data from the *Wall Street Journal* and *Business Week*.

20 For a careful consideration of the shrinking role of middle managers in corporate America, see Raghuram Rajan and Julie Wulf, "The Flattening Firm: Evidence from Panel Data on the Changing Nature of Corporate Hierarchies," *National Bureau of*

Economic Research Working Papers, no. 9633 (2003), http://www.nber.org/papers/ w9633.

21 Paul Krugman, "For Richer," *New York Times Magazine*, October 20, 2002.

22 Krugman, "For Richer."

23 For further discussion of this relationship, see Leslie McCall, "Do They Know and Do They Care? Americans' Awareness of Rising Inequality," Russell Sage Foundation, http://www.russellsage.org/publications/workingpapers/knowcare/ document.

24 See Robert Putnam, *Bowling Alone: The Collapse and Revival of American Community* (New York: Simon and Schuster, 2000); Glen H. Elder Jr., *Children of the Great Depression* (Colorado: Westview Press, 1999).

25 Katherine Newman and Elisabeth Jacobs, "Brothers' Keepers?" in *What Do We Owe Each Other?* ed. David Rothman and Harold Rosenthal (Piscataway, NJ: Transaction Publishers, forthcoming).

26 The downturn in support for health care spending may reflect the timing of the last survey, which took place in the midst of the Clinton Administration's health care debacle.

27 A precise statistical test of this hypothesis requires additional analysis beyond the scope of this chapter.

28 Princeton political scientist Larry Bartels finds similar stability in other relevant National Election Studies questions over time. For instance, he finds that responses to "whether the government in Washington should see to it that every person has a job and a good standard of living" have remained relatively stable since 1972. While the average response has become moderately more liberal over time, the cumulative change over thirty years is only about 1% of the total length of the scale. See Larry Bartels, "What's the Matter with *What's the Matter with Kansas?*" *Quarterly Journal of Political Science* 1 (2006): 201–26.

29 Cybelle Fox, "The Changing Color of Welfare? How Whites' Attitudes Toward Latinos Influence Support for Welfare," *American Journal of Sociology* 110 (2004): 580–625, at 580.

30 Pooled data from the National Election Studies Cumulative Data File, 1972–2004.

31 See for instance L. L. Lemasters, *Blue Collar Aristocrats* (Madison: University of Wisconsin Press, 1976).

CHAPTER FIVE

Ballot Boxing | *Partisan Politics and Labor Market Risks*

PHILIPP REHM

LABOR MARKET RISKS AND
PERCEPTIONS OF ECONOMIC INSECURITY

The previous chapter by Elisabeth Jacobs and Katherine S. Newman explored, among other things, how aggregate perceptions of economic insecurity developed over time. This chapter investigates whether subjectively perceived labor market risks at the individual level can be explained by objective conditions in the labor market ("risk exposure"). It also looks at the aggregate developments of objective labor market risks—especially how risks are distributed across the income scale—and their political ramifications.

Regarding the relationship between subjectively perceived insecurities and objective labor market risks, it turns out that people feel economically insecure if they have objective reasons to do so. In order to see this, we can use the General Social Survey (GSS),[1] just as in the previous chapter. To get a measure of objective job insecurity, the Current Population Surveys (CPS),[2] a large labor force survey, was used to calculate the unemployment rate for each of over three hundred and fifty occupations, as suggested by the author in publications.[3]

A person's objective risk exposure, then, is the unemployment rate of her or his occupation. High unemployment rates, of course, are capturing a high level of risk exposure, and are expected to increase perceived economic insecurity. Unemployment is obviously not the only source of risks and uncertainties. People or their relatives may fall sick or become disabled, and so on. However, unemployment is a particularly tangible threat for large segments of the labor force and, as such, is interesting enough to merit further investigation.

When we cross-tabulate the perceived economic insecurity measure from the previous chapter ("I will likely lose my job next year"[4]) with the objective measure of risk exposure described in the previous paragraph, we find a very clear relationship between these two variables. The higher someone's occupational unemployment rate, the more likely she is to think that she will lose her job. Table 5.1 shows that the average occupational unemployment rate of those finding it "very likely" to lose their job is about 8.5%, which is substantively higher than the 5.6% for those who find it "not likely" to lose their job in the next year. The risk exposure for the more moderate answer categories ("not too likely" and "fairly likely") fall exactly in the middle (with 6.6% and 7.8%, respectively).

The GSS contains a variety of other items that tap subjectively perceived job insecurity.[5] The occupational unemployment risk variable predicts all of them very well. We can therefore conclude that objective risk exposure is a powerful shaper of subjectively perceived insecurities. But are labor market risks and rewards also importantly shaping other attitudes, such as policy and partisan preferences? The next section will argue and show that labor markets are, in fact, critical for understanding individuals' politically relevant preferences.

LABOR MARKET RISKS AND POLITICAL PREFERENCES

If you have to guess how a person that you do not know usually votes, and you can get only one "objective" characteristic of that person, which would you pick? That anonymous person's education, skin color, or age?

HOW LIKELY TO LOSE JOB NEXT YEAR?	OCCUPATIONAL UNEMPLOYMENT RATE
Not likely	5.6%
Not too likely	6.6%
Fairly likely	7.8%
Very likely	8.5%

Table 5.1

That person's gender, income, number of kids, or eye color? Perhaps you would like to know that person's political party ID or position on abortion. But these are not "objective" characteristics — they are attitudes or opinions, like a person's vote choice.

This section tries to convince you that a particularly good way to predict a person's partisanship (vote choice, party ID, party affiliation) is to infer it from her occupation. There are at least three main reasons why someone's position in the labor market is a particularly important source of preference formation.[6] First, the workplace is where full-time working people spend most of their waking hours. On an average weekday, an average full-time employed American spends about 8 hours and 30 minutes sleeping, about 8 hours working, and about 3 hours and 20 minutes for leisure and sports. The remaining 4 hours are used for household work, eating, shopping, and the like. Most of the leisure time goes to watching TV (about 1 hour and 45 minutes); less than 26 minutes remain for socializing — such as visiting friends or attending or hosting social events.[7] It is only natural that people's interactions with others, their situation in their job, their discussions with peers, and so on, shape their ideas about policies and politics.

Second, and in more material terms, *different jobs pay differently*. It is well-known that income is closely connected to individual-level preferences, and the lion's share of income is derived from wages. Regarding redistribution and social policies, for example, it is likely that poor people get more out of the system than they pay into it, while the opposite is true for richer people. It is not surprising, then, that rich people tend to be skeptical towards these policies, while poor people are likely to be favorably disposed to them.

Besides working environment and pay, there is a third crucial aspect of occupations that make them an important source of preference formation: the certainty they provide, or the uncertainty they bring with them. One easy way to think about the *risk aspects of jobs* is to consider future employment as future income. If someone loses his job and either becomes unemployed or is forced to take a worse job, this is equivalent to losing or at least reducing his income. Even if an individual has a well-paying job at the moment and is relatively well-off in the present, she may lose her job and be worse off in the future. Almost regardless of their income, people do care about this risk. Not only are they aware of this risk (as shown above), but it also shapes their social policy and partisan preferences. This means that even rich people can be expected to be supportive of liberal social policies if they have a risk of needing them in the future.[8]

In what follows, let us concentrate on the two latter aspects of occupations that are expected to have a meaningful impact on an individual's attitudes: income and risk exposure. Of course, these are not the only factors that influence how someone thinks and feels about policies and politics.[9] Other important sources are, for example, an individual's parents and her upbringing, or religion. In addition, not everybody participates in the labor market, and not everybody works full time. There is no need to downplay factors beyond labor markets that shape attitudes, but labor markets are an area we can systematically think and theorize about, and they are important for almost everybody in a society — unlike, say, churches. Even most of the (relatively) few who are not part of the labor force still depend on someone who is.

Different attitudes toward social policy predictably translate into different partisan preferences. A person with leftist economic preferences tends to vote for the Democratic Party. Someone with conservative social policy preferences is, in contrast, more likely to support the Republicans. This closes the circle between an individual's labor market insertion and her partisan preferences: her job shapes her attitudes toward social policy — via the working environment, income, and risk exposure — which, in turn, have an impact on partisan preferences.

Of course, everybody knows someone who has a well-paying job and votes for the Democrats. Similarly, some poor people do vote for the Republican Party. Thomas Frank's book *What's the Matter with Kansas* provides many examples along these lines.[10] However, once we abstract from hand-picked examples and focus on large trends, we obtain a more accurate picture. For example, Larry Bartel's review of Frank's book shows that anecdotic evidence may well lead observers astray.[11] You will lose money if you keep betting against someone who picks a person's occupation to predict partisan preferences, while you pick some other objective characteristic!

Let us now turn to the data. As above, we can again use the GSS, and the occupational unemployment rate variable derived from the CPS. A survey item tapping respondents' attitudes toward redistribution can

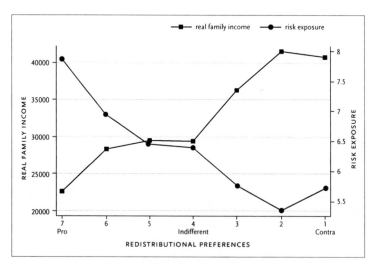

Figure 5.1 Redistributional preferences, by income and risk exposure

serve as a summary for a variety of different social policy preferences. In the GSS, interviewees were asked the following question:

> Some people think that the government in Washington ought to reduce income differences between the rich and the poor, perhaps by raising the taxes of wealthy families or by giving income assistance to the poor. Others think that the government should not concern itself with reducing this income difference between the rich and the poor. Here is a card with a scale from 1 to 7. Think of a score of [7] as meaning that the government ought to reduce the income differences between rich and poor, and a score of [1] meaning that the government should not concern itself with reducing income differences. What score between 1 and 7 comes closest to the way you feel?

The surveys also report a respondent's income.[12] Figure 5.1 shows how redistributional preferences go hand in hand with income and risk exposure (as measured by the occupational unemployment rates derived from the CPS).[13] The horizontal axis indicates the seven answer categories from the survey item tapping redistribution attitudes. At the very left, the 7 stands for pro-redistributional positions ("the government ought to reduce the income differences between rich and poor"); at the very right end of the horizontal axis, the 1 stands for attitudes against redistribu-

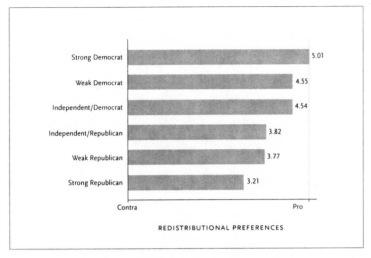

Strong Democrat	5.01
Weak Democrat	4.55
Independent/Democrat	4.54
Independent/Republican	3.82
Weak Republican	3.77
Strong Republican	3.21

Contra   Pro

REDISTRIBUTIONAL PREFERENCES

Figure 5.2   Redistributional preferences, by party identification

tion ("the government should not concern itself with reducing income differences"). The left vertical axis shows respondents' income, while the right axis shows their average risk exposure. The figure clearly shows the expected relationships: people in favor of redistribution policies are poor and exposed to high risks of unemployment; people who oppose redistribution are rich and enjoy low occupational unemployment rates. Labor market risks, the data clearly show, do translate into policy preferences.

Do these redistribution attitudes translate into partisan preferences? To examine this question, partisanship is captured by means of a standard survey item coding respondents into one of the following seven categories:[14] "Strong Democrat," "Not very strong Democrat," "Independent, close to Democrat," "Independent," "Independent, close to Republican," "Not very strong Republican," and "Strong Republican."[15] Figure 5.2 shows that social policy preferences — summarized by the redistribution attitude item — do relate to party ID. On average, people more favorable towards redistribution also tend to identify themselves with the Democrats. On the 1-to-7 scale, "strong Democrats" on average place themselves at around 5, while "strong Republicans" average at about 3.2. Given social scientists' general difficulties to explain individual-level behavior, this is an extraordinarily strong relationship.

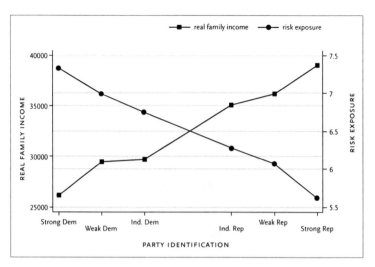

Figure 5.3   Party identification, by income and risk exposure

As a summary and shortcut, it can also be shown directly that income and risk exposure and partisanship are closely and predictably related. Figure 5.3, which is similar to figure 5.1, does just that. On the horizontal axis, six party ID categories are displayed, from "strong Democrat" to "strong Republican." The left axis shows real income, the right axis occupational unemployment rates (risk exposure). At this aggregate level, a perfect relationship between the averages of these three variables can be observed: individuals who "strongly" identify themselves with the Democrats tend to be the poorest and most risk exposed. The reverse is true for "strong Republican" identifiers, who are the richest and the least risk exposed. The labor market, and the risks and rewards it brings about, is a powerful determinant of policy and partisan preferences.

The figures show broad averages across all respondents and over long time periods. Do the shown relationships wash out when we consider more characteristics? It goes beyond this chapter to go into details, but they do not. Even when controlling for a variety of other factors that are known to be good predictors of partisanship (education, gender, race, age, region, church attendance, labor force, and marital status), income and risk exposure remain very strong factors influencing an individual's partisanship.[16]

However, it could still be that risk exposure matters more in terms of preference formation for certain groups compared to others. This is only partially the case. The relation between redistribution—and, likewise, partisan—preferences and risk exposure is somewhat stronger for nonblacks compared to African Americans; for men compared to women; for people not going to church very often compared to frequent churchgoers; and for people with low education compared to people with high education. Only regarding education are the differences substantial in terms of the interconnectedness of risk exposure and preferences. This makes perfect sense because education is an excellent way to "insure" against the risk of unemployment. People with high levels of education do not have to worry about job loss, and their (comparatively small) risk of unemployment should not be a powerful factor shaping their attitudes regarding social policies and politics. This is exactly what the data tell us.[17]

Averaging across all respondents, then, does not distort the findings presented above. It would still be interesting, however, to know whether and how the postulated and found links between labor market insertion and social policy and partisan preferences change over time. The next section will turn to this.

RISK POLARIZATION

The previous section argued that knowing an individual's occupation (and, therefore, income and risk exposure) allows for informed guesses about that individual's attitudes. But there is a potential twist. What if someone works in an occupation with below-average income and below-average risk exposure? Or someone with an occupation that pays pretty well, but also has a fairly high unemployment rate? How would we predict these respondents to vote?

The problem is that these individuals are cross-pressured. While one characteristic (say, high income) suggests that they should have conservative policy preferences, the other (high risk exposure) should make them embrace more liberal policies. They could go either way, and are fairly moderate when it comes to attitudes toward parties and policies. This section will suggest that developments in the labor market lead to a relative decline in the number of cross-pressured workers.

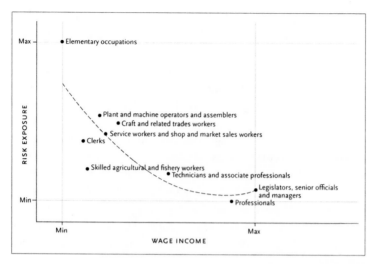

Figure 5.4

Over time, income and risk exposure became increasingly connected with each other. Four decades ago, knowing the size of someone's paycheck would not tell a great deal about someone's exposure to unemployment. Nowadays, knowing one characteristic allows for a very good guess about the other.

To see this, we can track a measure of the relationship between income and risk exposure over time.[18] To exemplify the principle, figure 5.4 shows the relationship between income and risk exposure for nine major occupational groups in 2006.[19] On the horizontal axis, each occupation's average pay is displayed, ranging from the minimum (for "elementary occupations") to the maximum (for "legislators, senior officials and managers"). The vertical axis displays each occupation's average unemployment rate, again from the minimum ("professionals") to the maximum ("elementary occupations"). The dashed line — which runs from the upper left to the lower right of the figure — serves as a summary of the association between income and risk exposure. Simply put, the figure shows that there was a strong negative association between income and risk exposure in 2006. Low values of income were accompanied by high values of risk exposure. High-paying job were also those with low unemployment rates.

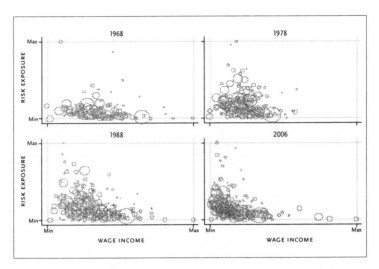

Figure 5.5

We can draw the same graph for each year since 1968, using the same definitions of risk exposure and income, and using a much more detailed occupational classification. For more examples, figure 5.5 shows the data for four different years. Comparing the association between income and risk from 1968 (top-left panel) with the association from 2006 (bottom-right panel), it can be seen that the link between these two characteristics has become much tighter. The graphs for 1978 and 1988 show that this process happened relatively gradually.

When comparing all available years over time (1968 to 2006), this finding is corroborated. Over the last four decades, income and risk exposure became increasingly closely correlated with each other. This can be seen visually (from figures that resemble figure 5.4 and figure 5.5); it can also be shown with rigorous statistical tests.[20] In terms of the betting game, this finding means that it is easier to predict someone's policy and partisan preferences based on her occupation in more recent years than in the past.

The increasingly tight association between income and risk exposure confirms Jacob Hacker's findings of a "great risk shift" in American society.[21] It does so coming from a completely different angle, using completely different data and a completely different methodology. There is no doubt, then, that something is going on in the American labor market. What are the political consequences of increasing income inequality and risk polarization?

POLITICAL CONSEQUENCES OF RISK POLARIZATION

The observable trends of increasing income inequality and risk polarization are candidate explanations for a variety of important phenomena. First, these trends suggest that the American electorate is increasingly "sorted out" into coherent ideological camps. "Cross-pressured" citizens—liberal Republicans and conservative Democrats—are likely to fade in numbers and importance, leaving only liberal Democrats and conservative Republicans. This can help to explain why politics has polarized so much over the last four decades. Second, the sorting process and increasing importance of economic issues may, ironically, be the reason why moral issues gain in prominence. Income inequality and risk polarization should lead to an electoral advantage for the Democratic Party, simply because the decisive voter should have moved to the left. This gives the Republicans strong incentives to focus on a second, cross-cutting set of issues—namely values (religion, moral issues). Third, the ever-increasing tightening of income and risk exposure may, again ironically, lead to a decline in the importance of risk exposure for partisanship. All three implications shall now be discussed in more detail.

POLARIZATION

In the last four decades, the American political landscape became increasingly polarized, at every level. By almost any measure, polarization at the elite level increased dramatically. Likewise, there is strong evidence of polarization at the constituency level ("constituency polarization"), i.e., signs of increasingly sharply divided constituencies for the Democrats and the Republicans. Furthermore, partisanship plays an increasingly important role at the mass level. Since the 1970s, the share of respondents who strongly identify with one of the two parties increased, while the share of pure independents decreased. Over the last four decades, income has become a better predictor of partisanship.[22]

As an example, figure 5.6 shows the increasing party polarization, as presented in Nolan McCarty, Keith T. Poole, and Howard Rosenthal's

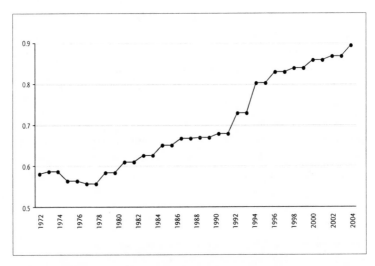

Figure 5.6   DW-nominate polarization [McCarty, Poole & Rosenthal; see note 22]

book.[23] The measure is based on a complicated statistical procedure that allows researchers to calculate the average liberal–conservative position of the Democrats and the Republicans in Congress. The distance between these average positions is displayed in the figure. As can be clearly seen, the gap between Democrats and Republicans in Congress significantly increased over time.

How did this happen? There are four main explanations for the increase in elite polarization.[24] First, it has been suggested that ideologically extreme activists have "hijacked" the political party apparatuses. Second, the Southern realignment led to sorting along party lines. Third, gerrymandering is said to have led to increasingly homogeneous constituencies and, hence, more partisan behavior of elites. Finally, increasing "constituency polarization" generates increasing elite polarization by "popular demand."[25]

Mass-level polarization has not been scrutinized as closely as party elite polarization. There are two main explanations for the "sorting" of partisans into more coherent camps, and this chapter offers risk polarization as a third explanation. First, it has been argued that mass-level change is generated by elite-level change: increased elite polarization comes with more sharply defined positions, which helps voters to sort themselves into ideologically consistent camps. Second, the book by McCarty, Poole, and Rosenthal draws attention to the fact that income inequality in the United States has dramatically increased over the last decades. They convincingly argue that, therefore, political preferences of individual voters should increasingly be related to their incomes, which should lead to sorting as well.

Third, as elaborated in the previous section, risk polarization (and increasing income inequality) leads to a sorting of citizens' redistributional and partisan preferences, resulting in more coherent partisan camps. Risk polarization, therefore, is a primary candidate for explaining mass and constituency-level polarization.

VALUES

Increasing income inequality and risk polarization suggest that the Democratic Party should have a structural majority for winning elections, at least if we follow mainstream scholarship in political economy. In that literature, it is assumed that both parties need to win the "median (income) voter" (one can think of the median voter as the typical swing voter who decides the election). Income inequality makes that voter poorer, while risk polarization probably makes her more risk exposed. Since, as shown above, it is the relatively poor and relatively risk exposed who vote for the Democrats, these developments should result in an electoral advantage for them. However, this clearly has not been the case. Why not?

In seminal contributions, John E. Roemer has argued that a party that is likely to constantly lose elections on one dimension—say, economic issues—has strong incentives to compete not only on that single, redistributive dimension, but also on a second, cross-cutting dimension (or cleavage), such as race, moral values, or foreign policy.[26] This is what Republicans should be doing, and this is exactly what many pundits observe.[27] The observed labor market dynamics (income inequality and risk polarization) help to understand why political competition in the United States not only gets more polarized with respect to economic issues, but also why moral issues become salient and polarized as well.

IMPORTANCE OF RISK EXPOSURE

There is a third, somewhat paradoxical, implication of "risk polarization." The increasingly tight association between income and risk exposure also suggests that the importance of risk exposure for preference formation decreased over time. Or, to be more precise, that the impact of risk exposure and income is increasingly overlapping. The simple reason for this seemingly counterintuitive result is that, once we know an occupation's income, we can easily guess that occupation's unemployment rate. The two characteristics are not independent of each other. Knowing both does not provide much more information compared to knowing only one. Thus, the observed pattern of risk polarization ironically decreases the impact of risk exposure on the formation of policy and partisan preferences. This paradoxical development is particularly bad for the poor. Not only do the poor become relatively poorer (due to rising income inequality), they also increasingly have to suffer from the vagaries of labor markets (due to risk polarization).

This chapter argued and showed that people have a good sense of their employment instability. Their perceptions of economic insecurity can be explained by the unemployment rate of their occupations. Moreover, the chapter suggested that labor markets are a crucial factor in understanding policy and partisan preferences. Labor market trends, especially the increasingly tight link between income and risk exposure, help our understanding of important political developments in the United States, including polarization and the importance of values in electoral campaigns.

What are the political implications of this chapter's findings? First and perhaps most importantly, voters care about risks in the labor market. Even if someone is employed in a well-paying job today, s/he may well be in favor of liberal social policies, given that s/he is employed in a job with relatively high unemployment rates. Second, the increasingly close connection between income and risk exposure suggests that it may be increasingly difficult to forge a broad coalition in support of social policies. Because the poor not only are becoming poorer but also more exposed to risks, and the rich are not only becoming richer but also less exposed to risks, higher-income groups gain relatively little from redistribution and are therefore unlikely to support it.

Increasing income inequality and risk polarization pose challenges to politicians running for office, especially Republican candidates. In the 2008 presidential race, Democratic candidates can easily adopt traditionally liberal positions on economic issues. Focusing on risks (i.e., campaigning against free trade agreements, highlighting the threat of offshoring, etc.) should pay off for either party to attract risk-exposed voters. For Republicans to win a majority, it probably will not be enough to exclusively focus on traditionally conservative economic positions (such as tax cuts). To attract additional votes, Republican candidates probably need to campaign on issues that are cross-cutting to the income–risk exposure cleavage, say moral and value issues (such as abortion or gun control).

Perhaps the most attractive topic, from a Republican point of view, is immigration. On the one hand, immigration can be phrased in ways that imply that immigrants take jobs away from Americans, which would be effective to win over some of the risk-exposed voters. On the other hand, immigration can also be phrased in terms of law and order — therefore attracting votes based on moral, not economic, considerations. The potential of anti-immigration positions to attract risk-exposed voters makes it a thorny issue for Democratic candidates, given that their social policy positions make them the more natural choice for these voters, yet traditionally Democrats have taken pro-immigration positions.

These considerations are not much more than informed speculations. A very different outcome, and one that seems quite likely at the time of writing (January 2008), is that American voters are tired of the ever-increasing income inequality and risk polarization, and the resulting political polarization. This would set the stage for a candidate who presents him- or herself as different from the political establishment.

No matter how things play out in the presidential elections, it is clear that labor markets and the risks and rewards they bring about are important for explaining the increase in political polarization in the recent past, and crucial for understanding political developments.

NOTES

Acknowledgment: I am very grateful for excellent comments and useful suggestions from Katherine Newman and Inés Valdez.

1   James A. Davis, Tom W. Smith, and Peter V. Marsden, *General Social Surveys, 1972–2004 [Cumulative File] [Computer File]*. *ICPSR 04295-v1* (Chicago, IL; Storrs, CT: National Opinion Research Center [producer]; Roper Center for Public Opinion

Research, University of Connecticut/Ann Arbor, MI: Inter-university Consortium for Political and Social Research [distributors], 2005). Yearly since 1975, about fifteen hundred respondents were interviewed face-to-face for about ninety minutes. Since the early 1990s, the survey is fielded every other year; about three thousand respondents are interviewed. For details on the GSS, see http://www.gss.norc.org/. The other obvious choice would be the National Election Studies (NES). Unfortunately, its occupational codings are difficult to compare with labor force surveys. Since this is critical for the analysis below, the reported data refer to the GSS survey. However, all results hold up with the NES data.

2   Miriam King, Steven Ruggles, Trent Alexander, Donna Leicach, and Matthew Sobek, *Integrated Public Use Microdata Series, Current Population Survey: Version 2.0. [Machine-Readable Database]* (Minneapolis, MN: Minnesota Population Center [producer and distributor], 2004). For details on the CPS, see http://www.bls.gov/cps/. The March Annual Demographic Files were used for the calculations.

3   Philipp Rehm, "Citizen Support for the Welfare State: Determinants of Preferences for Income Redistribution," Discussion Paper SP II 2005-02, Wissenschaftszentrum Berlin, 2005, http://papers.ssrn.com/sol3/papers.cfm?abstract_id=670761; "Who Supports the Welfare State? Determinants of Preferences Concerning Redistribution," in *Social Justice, Legitimacy and the Welfare State*, ed. Steffen Mau and Benjamin Veghte (Aldershot: Ashgate Publishing Ltd., 2007) and "Risks and Redistribution. An Individual-Level Analysis," *Comparative Political Studies* (forthcoming).

4   "Thinking about the next twelve months, how likely do you think it is that you will lose your job or be laid off?" [JOBLOSE] Answer categories are 1 "Not likely"; 2 "Not too likely"; 3 "Fairly likely"; and 4 "Very likely" (categories are reversed). The sample is restricted to full-time employed, N=11,593 (1977–2004).

5   In particular, the GSS data include six items that proxy perceived job security in a relatively straightforward way:

- Thinking about the next twelve months, how likely do you think it is that you will lose your job or be laid off—very likely, fairly likely, not too likely, or not at all likely? [JOBLOSE; N=13,960]
- Would you please look at this card and tell me which one thing on this list you would most prefer in a job? No danger of being fired [JOBSEC; N=9,916]
- Now I'm going to read you another list of statements about your main job. For each, please tell me if the statement is very true, somewhat true, not too true, or not at all true with respect to the work you do. The job security is good. [JOBSECOK; N =1,658]

- Please respond to the following statements based on your experience during the past twelve months unless otherwise specified, with reference to your current place of employment only. At work, job security is good. (Answer categories: very true; somewhat true; not too true; not at all true) [GDJOBSEC; N=1,604]
- For each statement about your main job below, please circle one code to show how much you agree or disagree that it applies to your job. My job is secure. [RSECJOB =1,480]
- On the following list there are various aspects of jobs. Please circle one number to show how important you personally consider it is in a job: Job security. (Answer categories: very important; important; neither important nor unimportant; not important; not important at all) [SECJOB; N=1,543]

When regressing each of these perceived job security variables on occupational unemployment rates (the samples were restricted to those in employment) and a set of year dummies, it turns out that people who feel that their job is insecure are likely to be employed in occupations with high unemployment rates, i.e., objective risk exposure is a significant predictor of subjective job insecurity in all of these cases.

6 See also, Kay Lehman Schlozman, Nancy Burns, and Sidney Verba, "'What Happened at Work Today?' A Multistage Model of Gender, Employment, and Political Participation," *The Journal of Politics* 61, no. 1 (1999): 29–53.

7 Data refer to 2005, and are taken from Bureau of Labor Statistics, United States Department of Labor, *American Time Use Survey—2005 Results Announced by BLS*, 2006, http://www.bls.gov/news.release/pdf/atus.pdf, tables 4, 8, 11. All data used in this chapter are publicly available.

8 The literature on social insurance and the welfare state uses this type of logic. See, for example, Hal R. Varian, "Redistributive Taxation as Social Insurance," *Journal of Public Economics* 14 (1980): 49–68; Hans-Werner Sinn, "A Theory of the Welfare State," *Scandinavian Journal of Economics* 97, no. 4 (1995): 495–526 and "Social Insurance, Incentives and Risk Taking," *International Tax and Public Finance* 3 (1996): 259–80; Karl O. Moene and Michael Wallerstein, "Inequality, Social Insurance, and Redistribution," *American Political Science Review* 95, no. 4 (2001): 859–74.

9 Recent reviews of the large literature on determinants of partisanship are Morris P. Fiorina, "Voting Behavior," in *Perspectives on Public Choice. A Handbook*, ed. Dennis C. Mueller (Cambridge, MA: Cambridge University Press, 1997), 391–414 and "Parties and Partisanship: A 40-Year Retrospective" *Political Behavior* 24, no. 2 (2002): 93–115; Harold D. Clarke and Marianne C. Stewart, "The Decline of Parties in the Minds of Citizens," *Annual Review of Political Science* 1, no. 1 (1998): 357–78;

Richard Johnston, "Party Identification: Unmoved Mover or Sum of Preferences?" *Annual Review of Political Science* 9, no. 1 (2006): 329–51.

10 Thomas Frank, *What's the Matter with Kansas? How Conservatives Won the Heart of America* (New York: Metropolitan Books, 2004).

11 Larry M. Bartels, "What's the Matter with *What's the Matter with Kansas?*" *Quarterly Journal of Political Science*, no. 1 (2006): 201–26.

12 Family income is used as the income variable. Wage income could be used instead, with the same results.

13 The following figures display averages across all respondents with non-missing values. The number of respondents and the covered years are: figure 5.1, N=18,857 (1978–2004); figure 5.2, N=19,127 (1978–2004); figure 5.3, N=32,907 (1972–2004).

14 Respondents were asked the following standard party identification question(s):

"Generally speaking, do you usually think of yourself as a Republican, Democrat, Independent, or what?" If they answered "Republican" or "Democrat," they were asked: "Would you call yourself a strong (Republican / Democrat) or not very strong (Republican / Democrat)?" If a respondent answered "Independent," "no preference," or "other," the follow-up question reads: "Do you think of yourself as closer to the Republican or Democratic Party?" to which they could answer "Republican," "Democratic," or "Neither." The answers to these questions can be coded into a partisanship variable, classifying people into one of the following seven categories (otherwise, they are assigned a missing value and dropped from the analyses): "Strong Democrat," "Not very strong Democrat," "Independent, close to Democrat," "Independent," "Independent, close to Republican," "Not very strong Republican," and "Strong Republican."

Despite some minor coding issues, this variable is comparable across time; see "GSS Methodological Report 56" at http://webapp.icpsr.umich.edu/GSS/rnd1998/reports/m-reports/meth56.htm.

15 When using the NES data, vote choice can be used as the measure of partisanship; the results do not change.

16 The evidence presented in this chapter is based on cross-sectional data; respondents were interviewed only once. This type of data does not track individuals over time to see how they change their attitudes when their income or risk exposure changes. Some of the NES do have a so-called panel structure, i.e., do allow for tracking respondents over time. From this data, we can see that individuals do change their partisanship quite frequently. Unfortunately, it is not possible to do

a very exact test of the conjecture that income and risk exposure shape partisanship, because of data limitations. However, some second-best tests reveal evidence along the lines of the cross-sectional evidence and render further support for the conjectured relationships. For example, it can be shown that respondents who switched their labor force status from employed to unemployed are disproportionally likely to switch their party ID to the left, while respondents switching from unemployment to employment disproportionally change to the right. For details, see Philipp Rehm, "Income Inequality, Risk Polarization, and the American Electorate" (unpublished manuscript, 2006).

17   These differences in terms of the link between risk exposure and other characteristics (gender, race, etc.) are somewhat offset by varying degrees of interconnectedness between redistributional and partisan preferences. For example, while the link between risk exposure and redistributional and partisan preferences is weaker for individuals with high levels of education, the link between redistribution and partisan preferences is tighter.

18   The data are from the CPS, and are based on very large numbers of observations (about sixty thousand per year).

19   Figure 5.4 is based on the International Standard Classification of Occupations from 1988 (ISCO-88), at the 1-digit level. This is for presentational ease only. The occupational classification used for the other analyses is much more detailed and distinguishes up to 387 different jobs; Peter B. Meyer and Anastasiya M. Osborne, "Proposed Category System for 1960–2000 Census Occupations," BLS working paper, no. 383 (2005). I am very grateful that they were so kind to share their conversion files with me.

20   When regressing income on risk exposure for each year and comparing the goodness of fit over time, a clear trend emerges.

21   Jacob S. Hacker, The Great Risk Shift: The Assault on American Jobs, Families, Health Care, and Retirement (Oxford: Oxford University Press, 2006).

22   On these developments, see the following publications: Geoffrey C. Layman, Thomas M. Carsey, and Juliana Menasce Horowitz, "Party Polarization in American Politics: Characteristics, Causes, and Consequences" Annual Review of Political Science 9, no. 1 (2006): 83–110; Gary C. Jacobson, "Partisan Polarization in Presidential Support: The Electoral Connection," Congress and the Presidency 30, no. 1 (2003): 1–36; Larry M. Bartels, "Partisanship and Voting Behavior, 1952–1996," American Journal of Political Science 44, no. 1 (2000): 35–50 and "What's the Matter with What's the Matter with Kansas?"; Nolan McCarty, Keith T. Poole, and Howard Rosenthal, Polarized America: The Dance of Ideology and Unequal Riches (Boston,

MA: MIT Press, 2006); John H. Aldrich, "Political Parties in a Critical Era," *American Politics Research* 27, no. 1 (1999): 9–32.

23 McCarty, Poole, and Rosenthal, *Polarized America*.

24 Useful reviews are K. Ono, "Electoral Origins of Partisan Polarization in Congress: Debunking the Myth," *Extensions* (Fall 2005): 1–8; Layman, Carsey, and Horowitz, "Party Polarization in American Politics"; Morris P. Fiorina, Samuel J. Abrams, and Jeremy C. Pope, *Culture War? The Myth of a Polarized America* (New York: Pearson Longman, 2004). See also the following contributions on polarization: Jacobson,"Partisan Polarization in Presidential Support"; William A. Galston and Pietro S. Nivola, "Defying the Problem," in *Red and Blue Nation? Characteristics and Causes of America's Polarized Politics*, ed. Pietro S. Nivola and David W. Brady (Washington, DC: Brookings Institution Press and the Hoover Institution, 2006), 1–47; Matthew Levendusky, "The Sorting of the American Electorate," paper presented to the American Politics Workshop, Yale University, 2007; M. J. Hetherington, "Resurgent Mass Partisanship: The Role of Elite Polarization," *American Political Science Review* 95, no. 3 (2002): 619–31; Fiorina, "Parties and Partisanship"; McCarty, Poole, and Rosenthal, *Polarized America*.

25 All of these explanations seem plausible, although it is likely that each of them alone explains only part of the trend. For example, gerrymandering would not explain the increasing polarization in the Senate, and redistricting explains less than often assumed. Likewise, ideological divergence along party lines can be observed for House members and senators from the non-South region, limiting the explanatory power of the realignment conjecture. See Ono, "Electoral Origins of Partisan Polarization in Congress."

26 John E. Roemer, "Why the Poor Do Not Expropriate the Rich: An Old Argument in New Garb," *Journal of Public Economics* 70, no. 3 (1999): 399–424; and *Political Competition: Theory and Applications* (Cambridge, MA: Harvard University Press, 2001).

27 But the literature is divided over the question whether moral issues became more important or not. See the debate between Thomas Frank and Larry Bartels, or Fiorina, Abrams, and Pope, *Culture War.*

Contributors

SHELDON DANZIGER is the Henry J. Meyer Distinguished University Professor of Public Policy, codirector of the National Poverty Center, and director of the Ford Foundation Program on Poverty and Public Policy at the Gerald R. Ford School of Public Policy, University of Michigan. He is a fellow of the American Academy of Arts and Sciences, a member of the MacArthur Foundation Research Network on Transitions to Adulthood and a 2008 John Simon Guggenheim Foundation Fellow. He is the coauthor of *America Unequal* and *Detroit Divided* and coeditor of numerous books including *Working and Poor* and *The Price of Independence*.

HENRY FARBER is the Hughes-Rogers Professor of Economics and a research associate of the Industrial Relations Section at Princeton University, the National Bureau of Economic Research (NBER), and a research fellow of the Institute for the Study of Labor (IZA). He is also a fellow of the Econometric Society and of the Society of Labor Economists. Before joining the Princeton faculty in 1991, Farber was professor of economics at the Massachusetts Institute of Technology (1977–91). He has also been a fellow at the Center for Advanced Studies in the Behavioral Sciences (1983–84, 1989–90), a visiting scholar at the Russell Sage Foundation (2002–2003), and a member of the Institute for Advanced Studies (2006–2007).

ELISABETH JACOBS received her Ph.D. in sociology at Harvard University in 2008 following a year as an affiliate of the Government Studies program at the Brookings Institution. In 2008–9, she will serve as the American Sociological Association's Congressional Fellow. Her dissertation, "Economic Insecurity: Real and Imagined," is a mixed-methods project that develops the concept of economic security by combining a large, nationally-representative, longitudinal dataset of American families and in-depth interviews with everyday American workers. With Katherine Newman, she is completing a volume on public opinion toward government intervention on behalf of the poor: *Brothers' Keepers? The Limits of Solidarity From the New Deal to the Age of Inequality.*

BENJAMIN J. KEYS is a Ph.D. candidate in the Department of Economics and a pre-doctoral trainee at the Population Studies Center at the University of Michigan. He received his B.A. in economics and political science from Swarthmore College, and previously worked as a senior research assistant at the Brookings Institution. Keys is a recipient of the University of Michigan's Rackham Pre-Doctoral Fellowship and the Department of Education's Jacob K. Javits Fellowship. His research interests include labor economics, consumer finance, behavioral economics, and housing and financial opportunities of the poor.

KATHERINE S. NEWMAN is the Malcolm Forbes Class of 1941 Professor of Sociology and Public Affairs and the director of the Institute of International and Regional Studies at Princeton University. She is the author of eight volumes on the economic fortunes of America's middle classes and the working poor, including her most recent book (coauthored with Victor Tan Chen), *The Missing Class: Portraits of the Near Poor in America.* With Elisabeth Jacobs, she is currently completing a volume on public opinion toward government intervention on behalf of the poor: *Brothers' Keepers? The Limits of Solidarity From the New Deal to the Age of Inequality.*

PHILIPP REHM recently received a Ph.D. from the Department of Political Science at Duke University. His areas of interest include comparative political economy (of advanced industrialized countries), political behavior, and labor markets. Philipp's dissertation explores the impact of labor market dynamics on individuals' social policy preferences. It also analyzes how these social policy preferences translate into actual social policy outcomes. After a stay at Nuffield College (Oxford University) as a Post-Doctoral Prize Research Fellow, Philipp will join the Department of Political Science at Ohio State University as an assistant professor.

ANN HUFF STEVENS is associate professor of economics at the University of California, Davis, and a faculty research fellow with the National Bureau of Economic Research. She received her Ph.D. in economics in 1995 from the University of Michigan, and has published numerous articles on poverty, job loss, labor market turnover, and retirement. Her current research includes investigations of the contribution of earnings inequality to the evolution of retirement wealth, and the causal role of income in determining children's labor market success and educational achievement.

Printed in the United States
144343LV00001B/1/P

9 780231 146043

DATE DUE